Safari Chronicles
VOLUME II

The Ancient Library

by
Rick Butts

Dear DAVEN,
Thank you so much
for your enthusiastic
support!
Mary Christmas —

Dec 2002

Dear Darren!
Thank you so much
for your enthusiasts &
support! Merry Christmas —
Merry Christmas

Dec 2002

Safari Chronicles Volume II
The Ancient Library

by

Rick Butts

Copyright © 2003

Publishers:

http://www.RickButts.com
800-442-6214
480-596-2691
http://www.SafariChronicles.com

ISBN: 0-9660981-2-9

Rick Butts.com LLC

DEDICATION

This book is dedicated to the amazing music and life of Rich Mullins.

There are millions of hues and shades in all the colors in the rainbow. In my lifetime, there are a couple fewer for Rich's early departure from this planet.

http://www.kidbrothers.net/

Other Treasures By Rick Butts

The Safari Chronicles Vol 1
http://www.SafariChronicles.com

The Big Butts of Life
http://www.RickButts.com/successtools

Kickin' the Big Butts of Life LIVE - Audio and Video
http://www.RickButts.com/successtools

Customer Service Goldmine
http://www.CustomerServiceVideos.com/ebook

http://www.eBookSource.com

http://www.ZapTheGap.com

For more information 800-442-6214.

THANK YOU

I am in great debt to the two most challenging professors I ever studied under, Dr. Doyle Young – Southwestern Baptist Theological Seminar for teaching me The Three Ways of Thinking…one of the most insightful, brilliant, and helpful concepts I've ever learned and Dr. Tommy Briscoe for instilling in me the breathtaking beauty of the archaeology and that brain-torturing timeline of Biblical history that changed my whole world view.

A great thank you to Barry Ochsner, my brother, fellow musician, creative technology consultant, and friend. It was during our travels to Israel in June of 1997 that the Ancient Library was first conceived. Barry's original song, "Miracles", has so been a part of the inner flame in my life that I've included it as a fitting conclusion to this book.

This tale is a whole lot better for the insight and story advice of my wife, Meagan Johnson. Although I still wonder why she didn't take my last name.

Tina Ihrig, office manager, high-priestess of data, and fantastic teammate for catching all kinds of stuff, and making me look a lot smarter than I am.

Most of all, I owe a debt of gratitude to the scores of readers who emailed, faxed, called, wrote, and, in a steady stream for six years refused to let me off the hook to write this adventure. I humbly submit my efforts to you…you know who you are!

Rick Butts
Scottsdale, Arizona
December 2002

Special Technical Thank You:

Barbara McNichol
http://www.barbaramcnichol.com

Barbara is a genius of editing writing. If you are even thinking of creating a book, brochure or web site, do yourself a favor and contact Barbara before you commit to print!

THIS IS A SEQUEL

In the summer of 1996, I published a paperback book called The Safari Adventure Company - The Three Treasures of Courage. After selling out two printings, I added five new chapters and published it as a hardcover under the title The Safari Chronicles Volume 1. *The Ancient Library* is the sequel.

I did my best to write this so you could pick it up and enjoy it all by itself, but my advice would be to read the first book FIRST! (Volume 1 is a clue.) But, since patience is a virtue that few possess, and if you just can't wait, go ahead, dive in and have fun.

Okay, one hint. The first book ended with the main character, Jim, reading a letter from someone he thought he'd never see again. This book begins with what was in that letter...

Go on now, get going!

This Book Has Its Own Web Site

Please drop by http://www.SafariChronicles.com for photos, maps, updates and all sorts of cool stuff. There will even be a place for you to share your reviews of this book, and to communicate with other people who have taken the "safari."

Will There Be a Volume III?

Thanks for asking. Yes, I'm working on an adventure already. This one will be a whopper of a sea-faring tale about the search for a shipwreck survivor. I'm not promising any publishing date this time, but get on the list to be notified about the new book by email at http://www.SafariChronicles.com or send an email to:

mailto:update@SafariChronicles.com

TABLE OF CONTENTS

The Letter

The final chapter of the Safari Chronicles Volume 1 ended with Jim reading a letter mailed from Africa…here it is!

Dear Jim,

I was told they found you the same day they rescued me. After the panther jumped us, I don't remember much. The rescue team found me but you were not there…I feared the worst. Thank God you are okay! Got some nasty cuts, but no broken bones. Going to have a grand scar. The nurses in the hospital here in Africa are spoiling me rotten. Hopefully you haven't taken another job yet, because we want to offer you a position with the Safari Adventure Company. There is a training seminar in Cairo, Egypt coming up at the end of this month. A courier will deliver a packet that includes tickets. I will see you in Egypt. We're hot on the trail of an archaeological masterpiece that I know you will want to be in on.

Jim, don't miss this opportunity. The adventure is afoot!

Weinberg

Prologue

AD 46 Akrotiri, Island of Thera, Greece

Sylvus ran faster than he had ever run in his life. Down a narrow stone street, he slowed only long enough to glance over his shoulder to see if the soldiers were gaining. Clutching the long clay cylinder that held the precious scroll, he squeezed between two massive marble pillars into a hidden alley. The hated foreigners, those Roman dogs, were strangers to the city and would not know this shortcut. The time it would save in his desperate race could mean the difference between safety and a slow death in a forgotten dungeon.

He tucked the ends of the common linen robe into his leather belt. A few years ago he would have laughed if someone had told him he would trade his expensive purple silk for this. Yes, he had given up a lot to follow the Way.

Bursting out of the alley into the burning Mediterranean sun, Sylvus looked down the hill past where the green of the island merged into the aqua sea. The boat had still not come. Each day he waited for Justinius to arrive brought him one day closer to death and the destruction of his timeless mission. How much longer would fate protect him from discovery?

Starting to run again, he hurried across the ornate clay tiles and fountains of the courtyard. His leather sandals kicking up little devils of dust, he moved swiftly into the familiar rooms of his own villa by the sea.

Pulling back a heavy tapestry of the Grecian Olympic games, he edged sideways feeling the damp coolness of the stones for the lever that would open the secret staircase. Sylvus tried to stay calm despite the knowledge that if he stumbled or made one false move, the few seconds lost might bring his years of risk and work to a sudden end. The company of Roman soldiers was already noisily searching the rooms overhead as he descended the stairs. He could hear the crashing vandalism and stinging steel of their swords destroying his home as they shouted obscenities with his name. Let them have the treasures in my house, he thought. They mean nothing to me now. It would be an unthinkable disaster for these treasures to fall into the hands of profane thugs.

Curled from fifty years of difficult life, a ripe old age for the First Century A.D., his bony fingers held his balance against the stone wall that led down the spiraling tunnel into the secret room below. Breathing hard, he clutched the cylinder, slipped through the narrow doorway and turned to force the stone door closed. Sweating and grunting, he pushed with all his might again and again. The muscles in his arms bulged with the strain of unfamiliar exertion. Still the heavy stone would not move.

Sylvus stepped back and clenched his jaw. What to do now? The guards would eventually notice the passageway down to his hiding place. Once the door was shut, however, it would look like part of the wall. There was another decoy room ahead of it that should be enough to convince any visitor nothing was down here.

As long as the door stayed open, though, Sylvus was dead. Probably torn to pieces by wild beasts in the Coliseum, the latest terror of the diabolical emperor. Worse than that, he thought, the treasures he had sworn to protect would be taken and destroyed forever. He looked back at the shelves lined with scrolls and the little writing table in the middle of the room.

Sylvus took a deep breath and whispered a silent prayer. Digging his feet into the hard dirt floor he turned again to the door with every ounce of strength he could find. He felt it give. Slowly it budged, then slid along, heavy, but free. The scraping sound of the stone stopped as it lodged in its final resting place.

The old man wiped the perspiration from his head on his forearm and unconsciously wiped his arm on his tunic. Collapsing in the small wooden chair by the writing table, he lit an extra candle from the lamp. The fat in the candle crackled and sputtered and slowly threw its warm yellow light on the amazing surroundings.

Sylvus smiled and nodded his head in satisfaction. He lifted the candle to check his provisions. Over the last few months he had carefully laid up a supply of food and water. He had calculated it would last him for up to three months. His plan was to lay low for a few days then seal the room and take passage on a boat for Smyrna. There, he would be safe to join his faithful friends and wait for the political climate to change. Then these bloody Roman dogs would get their just due.

There was never a trip he made that he did not take time to check on the most unique painting in the collection. The soft linen cloth slipped easily off its frame. All the work, all the risk, was worth it to protect such a piece. He lifted the lamp high enough to see but far enough away to protect the artwork from the oil that sometimes spattered out. He let the picture inspire and comfort him one more time.

Even before his breathing returned to normal, he could feel a deep rumbling in the tidy chamber. The walls shook and a thin veil of dust showered from the ceiling. The carefully sorted scrolls and jars began to vibrate and rattle across the wooden shelves before falling onto the floor. Cracking, shattering noises smacked all around him. The lamp danced across the table, fell off and went out. Gripping his candle, Sylvus bent his legs to maintain his balance. Terrified, he shuffled to the middle of the room where nothing could fall on him except the ceiling itself. He looked up in the darkness wondering if it could actually collapse.

Noise and smoke from Santorini, the island volcano was not uncommon. It hadn't erupted in the memory of any living Greek. He knew if he waited patiently, the room would be still once again. At least it would interrupt the pagan soldiers in his stolen house. The superstitious Romans still attributed nature's restlessness to the mood of their pagan gods. He settled down at the writing table as the slow rumbling continued. Pulling the inkpot and sharpened reed he used for a pen, he unrolled a scroll from the desk to the place he had left off and began to write again.

As he painted and scratched his account of the amazing events he alone had witnessed, the ominous smoking mountain at the edge of town blew its top in a giant explosion. It spewed millions of tons of burning rock in a rain of death on the citizens below. Ten generations of Greek families had lived since the last major eruption. Santorini seemed hell bent on making up for its long slumber. A slow river of fire would flow down the sides of the fractured black mountain and pour four-and-a-half feet of molten rock magma over Sylvus' house. Down to the sea it would creep, sealing him and the greatest archaeological mystery of all time in a silent tomb of darkness.

Kalil

Kalil descended the staircase of his opulent Libyan villa slowly and gracefully. He admired himself and his silk suit in the long gilded-frame mirror on the wall across from the grand staircase. Taking a gold foil-wrapped candy from a silver dish on its own table at the bottom of the stairs, he unwrapped it and slipped the wrapper in his pocket.

Any antiquities student would recognize the ornate emblem on the silver dish, identifying it as a rare Persian piece stolen from the Baghdad collection. Instead of gracing the museum where it belonged, though, it was only a common candy dish here, part of Kalil's personal furnishings.

He had come a long way from his boyhood deprivation. Each time he acquired an ancient relic and sold it for millions, and each time he enjoyed the comforts of his massive wealth, he consciously threw it up to the memory of his stupid dead father. He was living to pay back his rotten childhood. And, there was no end to the debt.

Growing up in the slums of New Delhi, he had learned to take care of himself. How he hated his father for blindly following his pious religion while his mother, four brothers and six sisters had lived in squalor and disease the wealthy looked down on them with disdain. Two of his siblings died young for want of treatment any wealthy nobleman could easily afford. Consequently, Kalil rejected his parent's religion and their lives.

Setting out on his own, he lived in Israel, Syria, and Lebanon, taking odd jobs and trying to make a living as a truck driver. He experienced the prejudice of the Jews, then the Muslims, then the Christians. Kalil had no prejudice for any one particular religion or government; he hated them all equally.

Restless, aggressive, and angry, he fell in with a group of young men who pilfered pottery and other treasures they could pull from the abandoned digs (and some not so abandoned) at night, and then sold them to the tourists. "The selfish pigs!" he thought. They want to rob our land. Kalil overcharged them but charmed them at the same time. He hated them all, but especially the haughty Americans who came to his country and threw their affluence in his face.

The little band of thieves escalated their activities into Egypt to rob a site set aside by the Egyptian government. This time, their take was way above the level to which they had been accustomed. Kalil proved to be the clever businessman, finding wealthy people to buy the pilfered treasures for a tidy sum. He had discovered his calling.

As the stolen artifacts business grew, his companions began to mysteriously disappear. Their wives wailed in his office, asking for any information he might have as to their last words. Kalil shrugged them off as if he knew nothing, even though it was he who fired the bullet into their skulls and buried their bodies in the desert.

The business grew and the demand for new inventory raised the stakes. Sophisticated museum robberies were staged where elaborately detailed fakes were inserted in the place of the authentic pieces. Many still sit in museum cases, undetected to this day.

Bypassing the go-betweens, Kalil soon began to deal with the wealthiest and best-connected collectors in the world. Keeping their confidence, he earned uncashed favors at all levels around the world. That special chemistry of illegal knowledge of a crime and a favor done was better than currency in a Swiss bank.

Kalil grew wealthy and powerful. Maintaining a reputation of swift and violent retribution for real and manufactured wrongs, he eliminated all competition. If you wanted the best and rarest items in the world, you had to buy from Kalil!

Crossing the black-and-white marble floor of the wide hall, he entered a side room from a private back entryway. Stepping into his office, he paused at the desk to press an intercom button.

"Have you brought that little weasel here?" he demanded into the microphone.

"Yes, sir. He is in the waiting room," came back a rough voice.

"I will be right down."

Kalil turned the knob of a hidden door at the back of the office and descended a spiral staircase into a modern dungeon. The walls were smooth and cool cement, lit by fluorescent lights. Upon first entry, the dungeon's temperature provided relief from the heat of the North African desert. Reaching the bottom, he proceeded down a narrow passage until he came to a heavily reinforced stainless steel door. Many were the screams and pleas dashed upon that door. They died in silence in the dreadful place the guards nicknamed "the waiting room."

Kalil entered as the door automatically swung closed behind him with a solid metal echo. Immediately the frigid air conditioning, turned down intentionally, gave him a shiver as his eyes struggled to adjust to the semi darkness.

A single dim bulb clinging to the end of a strand of wire hung from the ceiling, a nice gangster touch, barely illuminating four henchmen dressed in police uniforms. They were "guarding" a shivering man wearing nothing but his underwear and strapped to an oversized wooden chair with leather belts. His wrists were tied down on the arms of the chair as though he were a king sitting on a throne. He had been doused with ice water.

"Well, well, well," Kalil began smiling. "What have we here?"

"Please forgive me master. I admit I made a mistake. It will never, ever, happen again. I promise you," the bound man begged.

"You must understand, young man, that when you came to work here we stressed the importance of following every rule to the letter." Kalil spoke as softly as a father lovingly instructing his son. It amplified Kalil's cruelty.

"It was such a small thing, Master, and no harm was done," the trembling man pleaded through purple lips.

"You see there; that is the problem. You think that forgetting to lock a door is a small thing. I suppose it is to you, since the inventory behind that door does not belong to you anyway," Kalil instructed. "But if someone were to open that door and steal the inventory, it would cost me dearly. It would ruin me and cost you all your jobs. Everyone would lose."

"It will never, ever happen again. I swear to Allah!

"But, Allah doesn't come to this room?" Kalil said.

"Please, please, don't do this. I have a family! Three daughters a wife and a mother who is very ill. How can a cripple support them?" The man sobbed as tears ran down his face and onto his chest. Mucous ran from his nose as he blubbered in terror. "Please, Master, have mercy on me?"

"If I bend the rules for you, it will only lead to the whole system falling apart. Thank you for being honest about your mistake but I am afraid I have no choice. Gentlemen, you know the penalty. Extract it now, bandage him up, and send him home." Kalil turned toward the door and entered the code.

Behind him the shaking man screamed as he saw one of the guards remove a stainless steel hatchet from the wall behind him. One pulled the struggling prisoner's hand out as far as it would go exposing the wrist pinned down on the wide wooden arm of the chair.

The scream was cut short with the clanging shut of the heavy metal door. Kalil avoided these dirty tasks. Someone must be in charge and someone else must do his bidding. That is the way of the world. He reached in his pocket and unwrapped another piece of candy. Placing it on his tongue, he savored the sweet cinnamon taste and tucked its wrapper in his pocket. Cleanliness and order was the way to keep things running smoothly.

Pandora's Box

Once you have opened Pandora's Box, you have two choices. You can either slam it shut and try to pretend you didn't see what you saw - didn't know what you knew - or you can learn to deal with the new reality it has released. Looking down at the journal he had been keeping, Jim read the lines he had written last night.

For a month he had been bouncing back and forth between trying to forget what happened in Africa and trying to remember the experience he'd had.

At age forty-two, Jim had worked for the same large company since college. Riding the same elevator, doing the same job, he had been living the Yankee Four-Step. Get up. Go to work. Go home. Go to bed. Get up. Go to work. Go home. Go to bed. Numbed by the routine, he had felt content to do his time during the week and seek relief on the weekends.

The world turned upside down when he met the Safari Adventure Company, an eccentric and unusual group of wealthy international philanthropists who took people on incredible exploration journeys.

With his marriage strained to bursting anyway, Jim signed up for the safari to Africa. Swept away by the power of the fascinating people and the adventure, he was propelled into a new orbit by the excitement of life. But right in the midst of this wonderful experience the joy turned to terror. His companion and mentor was nearly killed and Jim found himself alone, fighting for his life in the jungle.

The "Jim" they picked up off that dusty jungle road and loaded into the jeep, scratched and bleeding, was not the same man as before. He had a concussion from falling down a cliff and an infection from the cut of the panther claws that mauled his companion. He was deep in a fever that would have made him delirious if he had not been rescued when he was. As he grew stronger in the African hospital, ten thousand fairies from Pandora's Box began to circle in front of him.

Never again would he be happy in a nine-to-five job, they insisted. For it was here, like never before, that he had really lived. On the edge of terror, right in the middle of the greatest challenge he had ever faced, he felt more alive than any time in his life. The courage that came from facing his greatest fears and then acting on them now belonged to him. He no longer doubted his strength; he had acted bravely and even risked his own life to save a helpless girl from a murderous gang. He had stepped out in faith and now he knew for sure.

He had become so clear about taking a new direction in his life when he returned home to Colorado. But now everything seemed to force him to forget this new passion. Worse still, his wife, Tracy, was the chief influence.

She wanted him to go back to work doing the same thing he had experience and training in. It was logical for him to go back to management. This would earn him the best income and he was highly qualified for the work. That is exactly what most people would do; yet he didn't feel like "most people" anymore. The problem was, Jim had no intention of ever doing that work again. He wanted something completely different. He wanted adventure.

On the safari, he had decided to commit to loving his wife with all his heart and do his best to make his marriage work. He came home with the best intentions and had made a good start. Even so, things went back to "bad". She had even insisted his mother and father phone him about what she called his "mid-life crisis." For days they barely spoke. The tension was so thick in the house; it was as if everyone wore a big pink hat showing the words "JIM'S JOB?" in flashing gold lights.

Within two weeks, it had all come to a head. With the kids off to her parents' house for the summer, they finally had to face each other. He played the conversation over in his head.

"You have no shoes. You haven't shaved in three days, and God only knows how long you have been wearing that flannel shirt," she said, reaching out and flipping the blue-gray plaid of his un-tucked shirttail. "You look like Mr. Mom."

Jim pulled his hand over his face, scratching the stubble.

"You are demonstrating classic signs of depression," she continued.

"No!" Jim shot back. "The only time I feel depressed is when I think of sitting in a stupid office, doing a stupid job I hate."

"What are you going to do with the rest of your life?" she pleaded, "Run away from home and join the circus?"

Jim held back the anger that normally jumped to his lips, then looked at her and smiled. He loved his wife and wanted so much for her to understand. But he didn't fully understand himself.

"I don't know, Trace," he used the softer nickname hoping to calm her down, "it is just that I . . ."

She stopped him cold and announced, "Well, you'd better find the answer and find it quick. I am sick and tired of putting up with your narcissistic navel gazing and searching for your inner child or whatever loser life you are up to. It's a real world out there and it's time for you to grow up."

She spun around, swooped up her briefcase, and escaped to her office. The divorce papers she had drawn up before he'd gone to Africa were easy to refile. Now it was official. They were separated and, with not much to fight over, soon to be divorced.

The Sunday paper sat open to the classified section where he'd left it yesterday. The little blue circles he'd reluctantly made on the insistent newspaper glared back at him threateningly.

Ignoring the paper, he returned to his study and surveyed the clutter. Every chair and table was littered with books and magazines that had occupied his dilemma since returning from Africa. Philosophy, religion, science, and adventure stories peeked back at him from every surface. Each one had been started with high hopes, but few had been finished.

He needed answers. A verdict. A decision. Compelling as the spiritual awakening in Africa had been, Jim had returned to a social and material world of religious confusion. He was a practical man and demanded evidence. With Weinberg's Bible as a starting point, he had pursued his suspicions of faith by going to a local church.

The service had been dry and routine. The people were all nice enough but it felt more like meetings at his dad's Moose lodge than the answer to the existential questions of the universe!

Why are we here?

Is there life after death?

What is the purpose of my life?

Attuned to these newfound questions, he stopped surfing past the religious channels on television to take a look. Sadly, the first Christians he saw on television were shameless hucksters. The couple that hosted the regular program looked like Frederick's of Hollywood crossed with Hee-Haw. Their antics and sidekicks on the chandelier-gilded stage seemed a far cry from the carpenter's message. Other programs ranged from obvious "mail in your money" schemes to fierce tirades against a variety of subjects. Why, he wondered, did some preachers feel compelled to scream their message at the people?

He sighed, produced a small paperback copy of Jack London's *Call of the Wild*, and removed the bookmark. Soon he was in 1925 mushing his team of huskies toward Juneau. He could imagine the icy wind in the beard he'd need to grow.

An hour later, he took a reading break and went to check his e-mail. He had been communicating with Weinberg and was waiting to get a reply from his last message. The whole Weinberg thing was such a challenge to Jim. The chaos surrounding the panther attack in Africa and Jim's terror-stricken flight of the scene had been the source of many nightmares since coming home.

Ever since he'd heard that Weinberg was alive, he'd both longed for and dreaded the moment when he could see the fascinating Englishman face to face and finally gain closure on the entire ordeal. They'd kept in touch via email while Weinberg recovered in an Egyptian hospital. Now Weinberg was on to a whole new archaeological adventure and Jim was dying to know more.

He pushed the mouse in his hand on the icon for his email program.

```
Message To: Jim@SafariChronicles.com
FROM: Weinerg@SafariChronicles.com
```

My Dear Jim

I know how frustrated you must be. You are a good man who's just been through a quite difficult experience. You are going to get through this, you can be assured. You've needed some time to process what has happened to you in Africa, but you also need something new to occupy. Sitting at home reading all the time seems good to you because it's reflective and that feels like progress.

In the end, though, it is really only part of the answer. Endless reflection without action becomes a circle trapping our solutions in round and round thinking.

Jimmy, I want to offer you a job with the Safari Adventure Company. I've discussed this with the key people here and I believe you will be an excellent leader. You can blend your corporate experience to relate to business people with your newly found passion for growth and learning.

We are starting some operations in the States, and will be opening one up on Colorado.

As you can see by the information below, I cannot offer you the kind of salary and benefits you had in your former profession, but if you can see your way to join, I promise you will not regret your choice in a few years.

I want you to attend a very important training conference the Safari Adventure Company is putting on in Cairo. It is almost upon us.

Yours truly, Weinberg

Jim took a look at the job information. The salary was a big cut in pay, but benefits were pretty good. He remembered that Weinberg said the company was in good financial condition. If he joined up, he knew they would make it well worth his while.

He leaned back in his chair and thought about the offer. No, he couldn't do it. It was just too "out there" to consider leaving in a few days for Egypt and spending his time traveling around the world, out of reach of a phone. All those nights away from home. The whole divorce thing was going on.

Besides, Tracey would be furious. He smiled at what she might say.

Jim hit REPLY on his email program and began to compose a response.

Dear Weinberg,

I cannot thank you enough for your gracious offer. I would love to be a part of the Safari Adventure Company more than you know. But the timing is just not right. I've got a lot of things going on here like…

He stopped typing and looked around the room. What *did* he have going on here? He was reading and hanging out. Jim used his backspace key to delete the word "like" and was just about to pop a period there after "here" when the doorbell rang.

He scooted downstairs and opened the door. It was the Fed Ex guy standing on the front porch with an overnight package. "Are you this guy?" he asked, holding up the airbill label for Jim to see. "Yep," said Jim as his eyes shot up the to Sender box. S.A.C. was all it said, but that was enough.

"Sign here, sir," said the man in the blue and orange outfit.

Jim closed the door with his foot. He tore the tab off the cardboard envelope and reached inside, then pulled out the familiar ticket jacket travel agents stuffed airline tickets into. The itinerary had him on a flight from Denver International Airport to New York, then on to Cairo. There was even a Gold American Express card in the packet with his name on it.

"No, no, no, this is not for real, is it?"

But it was all there. Every detail had been accounted for including the conference brochure with photographs of the Hyatt Regency Hotel and a group photo of the members of the Safari Adventure Company with Weinberg's face peeking out from the back!

Jim walked up the staircase to his office a whole lot slower than he had come down. He looked over all the documents in the Fed Ex pack and noticed his email was still up on the screen. He walked up and down the hall several times. He went down to the kitchen and made himself a sandwich and ate it in front of the television in the living room. He surfed every channel on his cable system, even the foreign language ones.

"Five hundred channels and nothing's on!" he laughed.

He cleaned his dishes and went back upstairs to the office. He sat down at the computer and finished the email, then logged on the Weather Channel's web site – international section. Next, he walked across the hall into what was once the bedroom he shared with his soon-to-be-ex-wife. He swallowed hard and opened the door to the walk-in closet.

"Now let's see, here. It's hot during the day and cool at night. What should I pack for the Egyptian desert?

The Find of the Century!

Jim made his way into the cavernous ballroom of the Hyatt Regency Cairo Hotel and scanned the room for an empty seat near the front. A thirty-foot tall video screen came to life at the front above a stage. The presentation had not begun, but the man on the stage was talking to a bright green face on the screen.

"Can you hear me, Larson?" the face on the screen asked in an accented voice.

"Yes, can you hear *me*?" the man on the stage replied, his voice echoing across the hotel meeting room. "You sound great," he chuckled, "but you are very green."

"I am very clean?" the voice strained back in what now sounded like a Frenchman speaking English.

Jim waved to Larry and CJ, a married couple from Phoenix, Arizona he knew from the weeklong seminar he'd been attending. The days had been full of some of the most interesting speakers he'd ever heard training Jim and the others for the personal development retreats and seminars they'd be holding around the world. Larry motioned for Jim to come over to an empty single seat next to them in the center of the room.

"Sit down, my friend," said CJ, motioning toward the chair. "Are you ready for the big announcement?"

"I can hardly wait," said Jim. "My uncle used to take me to the museums and ancient sites when I was a boy. I always wanted to go on an archaeological expedition."

"Me too!" said Larry. "My mother subscribed to *National Geographic* magazine. I used to read every archaeology issue over and over and imagine myself shining the flashlight into King Tut's tomb for the first time!"

"Yes," Jim agreed. "Me, too, until I heard a talk given by an archaeologist from the University of Tokyo. It sounds as though they spend most of their time doing more janitorial labor than anything else sweeping with little brooms and dusting old pottery."

CJ nodded in agreement. "No thanks!" she said, "I believe I would rather watch an Indiana Jones movie than do what amounts to housework in the middle of the desert!" They all laughed in agreement.

"This is probably as close as I will ever come to a big find anyway," said Jim. A river of people from around the world moved along noisily through the doors to find a seat in the main hall.

Jim said, "You know, I sure expected Weinberg to be here before now."

CJ nodded. She had heard Jim talk about his mentor all week and was impressed. "I've never met him, but between what you've said about him this week, and what others have told me, he must be quite a guy. I think you will see him very soon."

"I can't help but feel his presence here. He loves the Safari Adventure Company so much," said Jim.

"I know he will be really excited to see you."

The giant video screen lit up again as the audio-visual crew attempted to re-boot the system. The lights dimmed.

"Hello!" The man on the stage greeted the live audience. He had blond hair, blue eyes, and a ruggedly handsome face that spent a lot of time outdoors. His Midwestern American accent rolled from under a khaki bush hat. "My name is Larson. I am the director of the Safari Adventure Archaeology Team."

The crowd applauded.

"I know you are all excited to hear about our most recent discovery. We are going to go live now, via satellite to our excavation area on the Greek island of Thera. Can you hear us, Toussaint?"

"We hear you very well, boss," came back the French accent over the speakers.

"Can you hear *me* okay?" the Frenchman asked.

The crowd murmured in delight at the unexpected live satellite feed. The camera panned the eye-popping sight of tents, jeeps, and khaki-dressed workers. On tables behind Toussaint sat pottery and pieces of jewelry. The crystal sharpness of video caught every detail. It was almost like being there!

"Yes, Larson, I hear you and see you on our video monitor. Isn't technology magnifique! It gives me extreme pleasure to introduce to you today Messier Harold Toussaint, the chief archaeologist in charge of the dig here."

The camera panned to a young blond man with small round glasses and large pearly-white teeth. "Hi there Safari members!" he shouted. "How's the air conditioning and food at the primitive Hyatt?"

"Harry!" A voice off-camera called out in a harsh whisper, "you don't have to yell all the way to Cairo; the microphone is right here."

"Right!" He laughed and raised his eyebrows to the camera.

The crowd inside the meeting room laughed along.

"Come in tight. Lets make this dramatic," said the obviously excited archaeologist. The camera operator moved around to get a better setup creating a dizzying lurch for the viewers.

Harold Toussaint's face filled the screen. Past his long gray hair pulled back in a ponytail, you could clearly see his supercharged gray-green eyes.

"Have I got some news for you," he began. "As we excavated this cave, unearthed from the eruption of the island volcano Santorini in AD 46, we found a deposit of jars unlike anything ever seen in this area." His tone of voice became formally scientific. The jars were estimated to be about 1900 years old but had come not from this or any of the other islands in the area. They are obviously Roman. See here?" He held up a large earthenware jar and poured water across the dusty artifact, revealing a brilliantly painted color scene from an ancient Roman courtyard. The murmuring in the audience in the hotel room grew louder as some recognized the work.

"We see it very well, Harold. Tell us what is so special about these jars," said Larson, playing along.

"Inside these jars were several scrolls written in a Greek language common to the Mediterranean about AD 50 to AD 100. Not a fancy language. The language of business and common people."

"What sort of scrolls?"

"Many contained things like shipping lists for caravans, inventories, and bills of sale. While I know it's not very exciting information for the public, it is a treasure trove for us. We learn a great deal about a society by how they conducted their business. But that is not what we are so excited to share. The most incredible find was in the last section, from a room far back in the cave." Harold sat the jar back on the bench and adjusted his glasses.

"I'm no expert on ancient Greek, so I will let our language expert tell the rest." With that, he motioned to someone off camera to join him. "Safari members, meet the lady genius of the expedition, Dr. Sara Einstein."

The camera focused on a striking woman in her mid 30s. Sara Einstein could have been a fashion model. Her beautiful, delicate features contrasted with the rough countryside and geeky scientists. Her jet-black hair was cropped short and swooped up with a styling gel. Playful brown eyes peered across her slender roman nose. Sara smiled a mischievous smile at Harold and then at the camera.

"Hello," she said simply.

The crowd yelled greetings enthusiastically at the beautiful professor. Many had read her work and knew her to be a brilliant archaeologist.

"I will be brief. It seems that a wealthy man lived in a city on the Mediterranean Sea. He became a follower of Luke, the first century physician who traveled with the Apostle of Jesus named Peter. As many of you know, Luke was a very educated man. He was trained as a physician and the author of a major portion of the New Testament, namely the Gospel of Luke as well as the exploits of the Apostle Paul and the account of the birth of the early church we call the Book of Acts." The restless crowd fell silent and listened.

"Now, we have only just begun to decipher the surprisingly well-preserved fragments. Remember, these papyrus scrolls have been sitting in a jar on this island for nearly two thousand years, but they tell an exciting story."

Dr. Einstein pulled a pair of reading glasses up from the straps that held them around her neck. "The man, Sylvus was his name, became a curator of the writings of the apostles. His position as a wealthy merchant allowed him access and travel as well as the money to procure the sacred items of the persecuted church. He collected the autographs of the gospels, the letters of Paul, and many other important artifacts. He hid them from the Romans.

"The Jews were the only religion exempt from the emperor worship required of all others in the Roman Empire. They convinced the occupying Romans that the Christians were not a sect of Judaism, but instead a radical threat to the sovereignty of Rome. That's why Romans began to systematically kill all the Christians they could find."

"That is when they used to feed them to the lions and kill them for sport in the Coliseum," whispered CJ to Jim without taking her eyes off the stage.

"Sylvus was wealthy and powerful, a respected business man in his town. When times grew more dangerous, he built a secret room under his villa to store the collection. He would trace the stories of the whereabouts of these items, then purchase them and hide them on the next ship bound for Greece.

"After the Apostle Peter was crucified upside down - remember, he thought himself unworthy to die like Jesus - there was a scramble to flee the Roman death squads. Sylvus, who was well connected to merchants around the known world, set about to secure the other writings before they were destroyed."

"That's not logical! Why haven't we heard of this before?" shouted a man from the audience at the Hyatt.

"Dr. Einstein, one of the people here has raised an important question. Any collection this large would have been mentioned somewhere else. Why haven't we heard of it until now?" asked Larson into the microphone.

"That is revealed in the rest of the story," she said, peering back at the audience over her reading glasses. "May I continue?"

"Sit down, let her finish Mr. Spock!" A voice came from somewhere amid the laughter and cheers of the crowd and the embarrassment of the objector who quickly sat down.

Sara Einstein smiled and pressed on.

"Sylvus kept the location of this, shall we call it, Ancient Library, completely secret for obvious reasons. He would be killed if word got out. Only his most trusted servant, a devout man named Justinius, and a few believers knew of its existence. They tell of a volcanic eruption that buried the city, wiping out any trace of the town. Justinius and company returned to the place where the city had been with a detailed map but they lacked the tools to make such an excavation of the volcanic lava. At the time of the writing, the Roman persecution was still quite strong and copies of the manuscripts had been widely distributed so they decided to let them stay buried until later."

"Excuse me, Dr. Einstein. The excavation of Pompeii and other volcanic sites never yielded any manuscripts. They burned too easily in the extreme temperatures. What makes you think there would be anything left even if you could find this so called library?" asked Larson.

Harold Toussaint interrupted and the camera bounced back to him.

"Actually, Mr. Larson, the later excavations of Pompeii went beyond the city that was around at the time of the volcano into levels below. There they found many manuscripts of leather and even papyrus. Far below ground, they survived the volcano. Sylvus's library was hidden in a secret room well below his villa and covered by an elaborate series of stone doors. It is highly possible, even likely, that the room is still sitting in the exact condition in which he left it."

The audience was now buzzing with excitement. Conversations broke out everywhere as the professor continued on with scientific information about the dig. Everyone wanted to know about the inventory list.

"Harold, can you hear me?" Larson called out.

"Yes, I hear you very well," he replied.

"We have been told there was an inventory list. Is that true?"

"Yes, there were several letters written by Sylvus himself. He was trying to get the map of the Library and information about its contents to another safe location. We have what appears to be a partial list of the items he was protecting. It is a shocker. It is rumored to hold an actual autograph of one of the books of the Christian New Testament."

"What does he mean by an autograph?" CJ leaned over and asked Larry.

"An autograph refers to the original document. The first version ever written and set down by one of the Apostles," said Larry. "No one has ever even come close to finding an autograph of any of the books of the New Testament."

"If I could only see this original document, if I could just know that it was true, that evidence would be enough to believe," thought Jim. "How can I get to this island?"

"There are practically no autographs in existence of any of the great works of history. The possibility is absolutely fascinating!

"Well, tell us what you found."

"For starters, the original autographs of the Gospel according to Mark, part of the book of Acts, Paul's letter to the Ephesians, and the mysterious missing first letter to the church at Corinth!"

The audience sat in hushed silence, understanding the unbelievable significance of his words. "Harold, what led you to search the caves for these manuscripts?" asked Larson speaking to the two-story high face on screen.

"Weinberg." Replied Harold. Jim sat upright in his chair at the mention of his mentor's name.

"Yes, it seems that while he was recovering from his animal attack in Africa, he returned to the first-century villa we had stopped exploring. He somehow came upon the map, contacted me, and we sent the team here at once."

"Where is Weinberg now?"

"He was supposed to be up here for the broadcast." Harold spun around and asked a man in a turban a question in rapid French. The man pointed away from the camera and up the steep hill that rose behind the camp. Harold instructed the cameraman to follow his indication. The camera panned up the hill too fast for the viewers' eyes to follow. As they adjusted to the dizzying effect, the picture stopped and began to zoom in on a lone figure back down the hill near the caves. Immediately the familiar face of Weinberg began to fill the screen. Cheers went up across the hotel ballroom. Clearly, Weinberg was one of the best-loved members of the society.

Jim swallowed hard at the sight of his mentor. Tense to know he would have to wait still longer to get the load of guilt off his chest.

"Weinberg," shouted the assembly at top of the hill, "you are on global television, smile."

Weinberg looked up and appeared to see the camera. His determined frown turned to a big smile as he realized the Safari Adventure Company was watching him in Cairo. Too far to pick up his voice on the microphone, they could see him give his trademark wink and a thumbs up. This time, though, his face carried a long purple scar from his temple down his face, disappearing into his shirt collar.

"That scar is going to be Weinberg's claim to fame," Larson announced to the audience as Weinberg's magnified face dominated the screen. " I have spent the last two weeks there and he brags about it constantly." Everyone laughed. They understood the sense of humor and love shared between the two adventurers.

"I have saved the best for last," Harold's words came through the speaker system clear and sharp. The camera returned to the archaeologist. "Sylvus tells us that the Apostle Peter had kept some of the personal possessions of Jesus himself. He had given Sylvus Jesus' walking stick, a bracelet he wore, and several scrolls of teachings Jesus himself had written in his own hand!"

"Surely you cannot be serious, Harold," said Larson. "No one has ever referred to Jesus writing anything other than once in the dirt! His possessions? We are stunned! If this is true, it would be the biggest archaeological find in the history of the world. The impact of this Ancient Library as you call it, would explode in the world."

Jim sat with his mouth open listening to this staggering report. If these artifacts were found, they would prove once and for all the claims of Christianity to the world. More importantly, they would settle once and for all the struggle in his mind between the claims of the Bible and the arguments of modern rational thinking.

Suddenly, the video and audio feed crackled with static. The picture wobbled and began to shake. A steady machine noise grew louder over the speakers. The scene behind the chief archaeologist for the Safari Adventure Company Archaeological Team Number Four revealed a strong wind blowing across the dig.

"Some idiot is trying to land a helicopter here!" shouted Harold. Behind him people were running to cover the artifact tables. The camera rocked as the image on the big screen began to break up with static and interference.

"We're losing you, Harold," said Larson, frowning at the crackling picture. Concern for his team was obvious in his voice.

"Oh, yeah, I almost forgot to tell ya," shouted Harold, now holding his hat, his blonde hair whipping across his round glasses. "The Library also contains a painting of Jesus made while he was still alive! Do you hear me? The first-ever eyewitness picture of the face of Jesus Christ in history! Do you believe it?"

"Harold!" shouted Larson anxiously at his friend, "can you get a shot of what is going on?"

There was no reply as the horrible scene unfolded to the stunned observers.

The sound of several rapid popping noises shot out of the speakers. The camera turned to reveal a small army of fierce commandos dressed in fatigues, leaping from an attack helicopter, and firing on the scientists and the laborers.

"Oh, my God. No! No!" were the only words from the invisible video camera operator.

Sand and chalky smoke swirled around the macabre scene. Through the rolling smoke and sand, a strange sight emerged as if from the fog. There, the shape of Dr. Sara Einstein stood clutching a light blue clay cylinder. Defiantly she held frozen, her back to the camera, facing the onslaught though bullets flew and exploded all around her.

The members of the Safari Adventure Company sat helplessly and watched the merciless attack. The video camera lurched and then fell on its side, showing only the boots of the commandos rushing by and the sound of popping ammunition and screaming.

The camera went dead.

The screen turned black.

The audience in the ballroom of the hotel sat in stunned silence.

A split second later, a deafening explosion rocked the ballroom and tore out the wall behind the screen. The force of the blast hurled instantly dead bodies of the people in the first five rows through the air and onto the laps of the people in the back. Shattered glass, metal, and chairs sliced through the room, tearing flesh and getting buried into anything unlucky enough to be in their path. The force of the blast blew out the back wall and shattered the glass doors all the way in the front of the hotel. Harsh, blinding, midday sunlight flashed into the once-dark theater like a flash bulb that stayed on, compounding the confusion of the survivors. They groped through the dust and smoke, instinctively running away from the pain they did not yet understand.

The Sign of the Red Arrow

When Jim opened his eyes, he was looking at the bottom of a chair. The chair disappeared and Larry's face appeared. "Come on!" he shouted, pulling Jim to his feet. Then he and CJ joined the race of survivors pouring out of the smoking ballroom. He ran through the chaos that used to be the marble lobby, away from the blast and toward the entrance of the hotel. He emerged through a veil of burnt-electric smelling smoke into the driveway, raising his hand to shield his eyes from the bright Egyptian sun.

Unseen elbows and shoulders jostled past him from all directions, moving on without apology. As his eyes adjusted to the glare, the sounds he'd been hearing began to connect with the emerging visual around him. Taxis were swooping up people as fast as they could load them, tires squealing as they hurried away. Some collided with each other in jerking attempts to race away in the aftermath of the shock. A dozen languages, spoken way too fast to interpret, pin-balled around Jim. He could make out only one thing: Everyone here wanted to get to the airport and out of Cairo, NOW!

Taking a step toward the curb to join the stream of differently colored cabs, Jim stopped and realized he had another problem. "Oh no, my suitcase and stuff." He turned around and faced the hotel he'd just escaped, looked up and tried to count the floors to where he imagined his room would have been. Smoke was pouring from the lobby. Orange flames reached out for oxygen from multiple windows on the second and third floor. Bluish-white streams of smoke were beginning to squeeze their way out of the fourth floor as if someone was running along and raising each window to let them out in sequence. Jim watched in astonishment at the speed and progress of the fire when he saw signs of its progress appearing in the windows of the fifth floor where his room was.

27

"Well, even if it's not already charcoal, it will be soon. Whatever I might get back won't be worth waiting for." He patted his pocket for his wallet instinctively. It was still where he'd placed it this morning. "Goodbye suitcase," he muttered then turned and sprinted toward the next car in line, a blue-and-white Mercedes caked in dried red mud.

"Hurry! Hurry! You must leave this area now!" the turbaned driver shouted and waved in Jim's direction. "I get you to airport very, very fast! Hurry! Hurry!" The driver made eye contact with Jim as the next logical fare headed his way. "Hurry friend, there is often another bomb, come right away." He held the passenger door open for Jim who dived in head and shoulders first landing on all fours into the back seat. Jim heard the door slam tight behind him. Pushing himself up with his palms on the seat he heard the door open again and felt two powerful hands mash him across the seat.

"Airport! Now!" a deep voice ordered.

Jim turned to react to the shove – then stopped short, astonished to find that his new seatmate was the man from the stage.

"Larson!" Jim said, "Man, how in the world aren't you dead?"

"You – airport – NOW!" Larson shouted again to the driver who had already slid behind the wheel and thrown the Mercedes into gear in one practiced motion.

"Hang on!" yelled the driver as he rolled over a curb and dodged three other vehicles, shifted and sped away from the hotel. "What airline are you on?" he asked his usual question.

"No airline – not commercial" Larson yelled again loudly. "Take me to general aviation. I have a jet copter there."

"Why are you yelling so loud?"

"WHAT?" Larson turned to Jim. The wide whites of his eyes stared at Jim out of a charred face

"WHY – ARE – YOU – YELL…" Jim stopped in mid-sentence when he realized the answer. He adjusted his volume and said loudly and slowly, "The blast must have hurt your ears. You are yelling really loud."

"Sorry," said Larson, still booming, "that bomb must have hurt my ears." Larson rubbed hard on both ears with his palms.

Jim gave him a quick thumbs up and a sympathetic smile.

The driver skillfully piloted the Mercedes through the chaotic traffic. Twice he rolled across a curb, then bounced roughly back onto the roadway. Ambulances, fire trucks, and police cars sped past them in the opposite direction.

"Hi, Larson. My name is Jim." Larson looked down at the bloody hand Jim offered.

"You are bleeding. Are you hurt badly?" Larson squinted at him.

"I'm not sure...I...uh...I don't think so. I think this blood is from a little glass cut. Not that bad. Not as bad as some of the others back in the hotel." Detailed memories of the explosion began to register in his mind for the first time. They would be there for many nights to come.

The driver rounded the boulevard and shot up a side street past a donkey-drawn cart and its driver. The cab again bounced over a curb and rocked back onto the main road. A sign with a picture of an airplane on it flew by.

"Where are you going, Larson?" Asked Jim. "What are you going to do now?"

"I am going to the island to see what is left of the dig and if I can help anyone there," he answered. "You ought to get the heck out of this city now. "Any members of the Safari Adventure Company are targets for crazy people."

"No, no, no, I was headed to the island anyway to see Weinberg. You have to take me with you."

"Hey, I know you," said Larson. "You are the guy who survived the poacher attack in Africa last year, aren't you?"

"Yeah, that was me."

"That was incredible. I was there, too. I was in the search team that found Weinberg."

"Really?"

"Yes, good to see you again." Larson shook Jim's hand with enthusiasm. "Weinberg has spoken about you many times." He paused, his mind jerked back to the excavation site. "Weinberg said you were coming, but I don't think it's safe now. You ought to get out of here, fast."

"Who is behind this?" asked Jim, changing gears to think of a way to get to the island.

The city sped by the window. Then Larson swallowed hard and faced Jim. "Not everyone is happy to see the doors of the Ancient Library open to the public."

The driver turned on the radio and found a station.

"The Red Arrow, a militant patriot group of Egyptian terrorists claimed to have set the bomb at the Hyatt today that killed 35 people and injured another 82." The voice spoke in perfect British English out of the Alpine stereo in the dash of the cab.

"Turn that up," said Larson.

"They are threatening to strike again if three of their group are not released from a foreign prison and returned to a neutral country by the end of the week," the announcer reported as the cab slammed into a crater in the road.

Jim rubbed his eyes and tried to focus. He felt the dried blood on his face and brushed a few dark red flakes away. They listened to the radio report.

"I am standing outside the devastated hotel as firefighters continue to try and control the blaze," the radio announcer shouted over the sirens.

"I cannot believe how fast it caught fire after the bomb went off," said Jim.

"In other news," the announcer continued, "the University of Cairo Antiquities Department reported the theft last night of several crates of archaeological relics recently unearthed from a university expedition dig near Thebes, site of the ancient temple of Karnak. The theft is the sixth such robbery in the last year in the Middle East. Investigators suspect an underworld smuggling ring."

"I wonder if they will report the murders from the raid on the archaeological site?"

"Probably not. At least not for a while," said Larson. "There is no way anyone local would be able to verify it. Remember, we saw it on an a private, closed-circuit satellite feed."

"Why…I mean, who would do such a thing? The news said terrorists; I think they called them the Red Arrow. It's a group of Egyptian patriots trying to run off foreign influences."

"The Red Arrow did not kill the people at the dig and they did not set the bomb at the hotel."

"Who is behind this violence if not terrorists?" Jim insisted.

"There are people who want the treasures we are seeking very badly. They are not honorable people. They are thieves. They steal artifacts from graves, museums, and private collections, and even rob excavation sites.

"What would they do with stolen antiquities? Where is the money in something no one could buy?" asked Jim.

"Oh, they have customers. They cannot sell stolen antiquities in any legitimate market. They have a very elite clientele who collect for their own selfish passion. They hide these treasures away in secret rooms for themselves and their friends. Heaven only knows how many of the most significant relics of the past are squandered away in the villa of some super wealthy miser."

"It's a shame," said Jim.

"There are also those who seek to keep historical artifacts from surfacing for religious reasons," Larson said. "Anything that proves the authenticity of the Bible weakens the power of certain rulers and leaders who rely on the oppression of the so- called religion of their country."

Jim began to glimpse the bigger picture. His world was CNN and USA Today - information he was spoon-fed by the U.S. media. This kind of international thinking was foreign, and very uncomfortable. It was easier not to think about world events and movements. Besides, what could he do to change things?

"Then the discovery of the Library would benefit both of these kinds of people if they could beat legitimate archaeologists to the punch, wouldn't it?" said Jim.

"Most of the people who would pay dearly for these treasures - be they collectors or religious pirates - would never soil their hands by directly procuring them."

"I don't understand," said Jim. "How do they get them then?"

Larson gripped the seat in front of him as the driver almost put the Mercedes on two wheels to avoiding hitting a motorcycle. He took a deep breath as if bracing himself to lift a heavy object.

"There is a devil in the world who sniffs out every major find," he said. "This evil man is extremely powerful with influential international connections bought with large bribes and favors. Worse than his power is his heart. He will kill, without prejudice, anyone who gets in his way. Even his own wife."

"No," said Jim.

"Yes. He shot her himself in front of his staff after he discovered she revealed some secret information, quite by accident, to a friend at a luncheon. His world is a secret society of paid silence," Larson sighed. Then he continued. "Okay, I know you are a member of the Safari Adventure Company and if Weinberg is hiring you, I guess it's okay to tell you a little more, considering the circumstances." Jim waited.

"The Safari Adventure Company is much bigger than you know. The company is involved in some sophisticated research and archaeology. We are over one hundred years old and funded very,

very, well because of years of investing and some extremely powerful backing members," Larson started.

"What's that got to do with helicopter commandos and blowing up the Hyatt?" "The existence of the Ancient Library has been rumored to be true for the last three years. The individual I was telling you about wants it, too."

"Who?"

"An antiquities thief named Kalil."

"He was obviously behind the raid on the archaeology site," said Larson, "maybe even there in person."

"Okay, there's a big-time thief behind the raid. What about the explosion at the Hyatt?"

"Same guy. Blaming it on the Red Arrow. Easy to get the media to run that."

"But, why?"

He *hates* the Safari Adventure Company. They have outrun him on the last two big finds. And he knows we are on to the Library.

The Mercedes taxi sped along a dirt road across a wide dune. A large Quonset hut appeared in the distance. A sleek high-tech helicopter sat next to it, with a half dozen men and women in flight overalls crawled over and around the chopper. In the next few seconds, Jim knew his opportunity would disappear forever.

Jim asked, "Let me come with you?"

Larson leaped out of the Mercedes and sprinted across the runway to the helicopter without looking back.

Oh no! He didn't hear me! "Hey, what about me?" screamed Jim as he jumped out of the doorway of the Mercedes. "Larson. I want to go with you. *Larson*!"

"You!" Larson pointed his finger and yelled right at Jim. "Go home!"

"No!" shouted Jim. Larson stopped and turned back to Jim. Before he could speak, Jim shouted, "I am absolutely not going home, "

"Get the hell out of this country. You are in way over your head, Jim," shouted Larson.

"Let me stay and help," Jim shouted back.

"What do you mean help? I didn't ask you to help me."

"I want to help you put the excavation back together and find the Library."

"Okay, man, are you an archaeologist?"

"No."

"Have you ever traveled in the Middle East? Do you know your way around the country or the customs?"

"Well, no."

"Do you speak any of the languages?"

"No, Larson. I am not the first person you might pick to help with the operation but your options look limited, right?" Jim snapped.

Larson rubbed his chin and looked back at the brick wall.

"I *am* a member, Larson. And I am an employee of the company," Jim said softly to Larson. This man had just lost many of his companions out in the desert and was under a lot of pressure. Jim was smart enough to try to balance his desire to go. Larson just started walking toward the hangar. Jim, hesitated, then followed immediately.

"You are going to need help. With the attack at the site and the bomb at the hotel, you don't have a lot of choices. I can drive a truck or shovel or make phone calls. Look at me; I'm six-foot-two and in great shape. I can carry stuff, for crying out loud! I am excellent with every kind of computer system and the Internet. I want to help and I am highly motivated." Jim's voice was firm. His eyes fixed on Larson as he hustled to keep up.

Still, Larson was silent while Jim recited his impromptu verbal resume.

"And...I went all the way to Eagles Scout in the Boy Scouts of America!"

Larson stopped at that and turned to Jim.

"What did you say?"

"You heard me," said Jim.

"You think I will change my mind because you were a Boy Scout?" he gave a half laugh.

"Eagle Scout."

"So, if I need some really sophisticated knot untied, you can do it."

"Okay, I guess so."

The blond American clenched his eyes shut and rubbed his face with both palms. "Aaaaagh!" he growled in frustration. "Unfortunately you have an excellent point. My troops are thin. I could use a smart hand."

"Great. I'm in," said Jim smiling and extending his hand. But Larson said nothing. He took Jim inside the dusty Quonset hut that served as a hangar and sparse dusty office, then shut the door to the howling wind outside.

In a quieter voice, he asked, "Why in God's name do you want to get into this helicopter and fly out into what you saw in that video screen? We might be shot right out of the sky before we even reach the site? What's in it for you?

"Larson, come on. She's ready." A technician in grease streaked orange coveralls shouted from outside.

Jim thought for a moment, then answered.

"When I first met you guys, I only really believed in one thing. Money. It was my God and my religion. I'm not a greedy person but that is all I trusted. When we went on the African safari, Weinberg and Benjamin shared their faith with me. Gave me the book *The Three Treasures*. The treasures of the mind, heart, and spirit rang absolutely true and I knew it.

"The Bible verses and the explanations made me very uncomfortable. I liked you guys and all, but I hated church and all that it represented."

Larson nodded, unsmiling. As the lead technician walked in, Jim continued.

"When Weinberg jumped in front of the panther that attacked me, saving my life and sacrificing his, I realized he believed the Bible totally. I knew his faith was real to him, but not to me.

"Since returning home, I have been torn in two. Part of me wants to believe, but the other part says 'you fool, be practical'. If the Bible is true, then most of the things I've relied on *aren't* true."

Jim stopped talking. The wind swirled a wave of sand into the hut.

"I cannot get on with my life unless I know the truth. I have to know if the Bible is true. The Library would contain that undeniable proof. If I can touch these treasures with my own hands and see them with my own eyes, I will accept every word. If not, then I will remain unconvinced. I think it may be my last chance."

At these last words, the lump forming in his throat grew larger and Jim's voice cracked.

"You are asking the wrong question," Larson said over the roar of the chopper as he placed a hand on Jim's shoulder. "This is not the way to solve your spiritual dilemma."

"When I saw the archaeologists talking about the Library, I decided I had to be a part of the search," said Jim.

"Our work will be unpredictable," said Larson, "If we are able to make any progress, we will have to work like dogs. I am talking about physical labor. And if Kalil is involved, we may be risking our lives to learn the truth."

"For God's sake, Larson. The man who saved *my* life was walking up that hill when they hit the camp. You have to let me go!"

Larson looked at the helicopter. The man in the coveralls waved urgently.

Jim turned and left the two men looking at each other. He grabbed the door handle and jerked it open, then jogged the short distance out to the helicopter, past the crew, and climbed up inside. He dropped into the passenger door and started fastening the safety harness. He strapped in just ahead of Larson.

As Larson gestured to the technician on the ground, Jim looked around and realized where he was. He was back in a helicopter. This is where the last adventure ended in Africa. It might as well be where a new one began. Jim jerked his straps down tight. No way will they leave me here, he thought. Not unless they drag me off this helicopter.

Death from the Sky

Through the swirling sand and noise spun off the slowing helicopter blades Kalil emerged onto the beach with the arrogance of a conquering warlord. His designer sunglasses reflected the piercing Mediterranean sun as he straightened his starched khaki uniform. He had landed in a second sleek black helicopter moments after the radio report from the first helo reported the success of the surprise attack. It had come as his pilot hovered near the scene.

"Hurry," he shouted, "we have only a brief time before trouble arrives."

The red-masked soldiers, feigning membership in the Red Arrow for any witnesses, had handcuffed Toussaint to the bumper of a Jeep. He glared up at Kalil as the thief strode by. The assassins now turned into laborers and began loading anything that resembled an artifact or field record into containers. Hustling them into the helicopters, they hardly spoke.

Kalil strode with cold disregard across the bodies of the cameraman and the worker who had made the mistake of lifting an ancient rifle from the jeep when the attack began. His worry was not the killing but the arrival of the wrong commander of the factious Greek military. Of all the schemes he had pulled as an international antiquities thief and smuggler, this was by far the boldest. His heart beat fast at the excitement, thinking about the daring raid.

If they could get loaded and airborne soon, he would pull this off. His helicopter was the fastest craft in the Middle East. Its stealth technology was unequaled outside the cutting edge hardware of the United States Air Force.

"Where is Einstein?" he screamed at the commander of the attack helicopter who ran up and saluted smartly.

"She is getting medical attention right now, Sir," the commander barked back over the noise.

"Damn you idiots!" Kalil swore, "I gave strict orders that she was not to be injured. We need her. She is absolutely critical to this mission!"

"She refused to hide. She stood right in the way as the shooting began."

"Who shot her?" screamed Kalil looking across the camp for her as if he could spot the offender. "He will be executed by me personally before we leave."

"She wasn't shot, sir," explained the commander, stepping back from his violently angry boss. "She caught a fragment from something and got knocked down. I am certain she will be fine."

Kalil looked across the camp and spotted the professor approaching with the assistance of two very helpful soldiers. He watched her as they hustled her nearer. Even from a distance it was obvious she was an attractive woman. Her short black hair spiked up like a rooster ready to fight. Her face was red with anger as she strode toward Kalil, her model's nose defiantly in the air.

"I was concerned for your safety, Dr. Einstein. Are you all right?" Kalil asked.

"You bastard, Kalil," her eyes were on fire. "This was totally unnecessary." The agitated smuggler instantly slapped her hard across the face. She cried out but stood back up and glared back into his eyes. Hands at her side, her light brown cheek revealed a growing crimson mark.

"I will overlook your outburst. You are just a little upset because of your injury." Kalil said smiling. He found it exciting to flex his power over such a woman. "You are lucky to be alive. I am sure you will feel differently as soon as you are treated to the comforts of the palace."

"Put her in my helicopter," Kalil commanded the soldiers as they dragged her away. The efficient attack team had loaded everything they could find and was now sweeping the scene for a final check.

"We have secured the area, commander," A soldier reported within earshot of Kalil. He was stabbing his weapon in the direction of the handful of researchers. They were tied together with strong nylon handcuffs used by riot police to restrain crowds.

Kalil made his way over to Toussaint.

"Do not make the mistake of lying to me, Dr. Toussaint," Kalil began.

"How do you know my name?" Toussaint asked.

"I have been studying your work. You are very talented, indeed. It is an honor and a privilege to meet you at last," Kalil replied.

"Not for me," Toussaint glared. "Take your plunder and go."

"Give me the map and all supporting documents, or I will be forced to terminate all future projects of yours."

"Terminate my projects?"

"Yes," said Kalil pulling a pistol from the black leather holster at his belt. He placed the barrel less than an inch from the French scientist's right eye. "If there is no more Dr. Toussaint, then there will be no more projects."

"Where are the maps, your notes, and the inventory scrolls?" he spoke in a loud, threatening voice. The helicopters had begun to rev their engines in preparation for takeoff.

"You have already loaded them into the big helicopter," said Toussaint through clenched teeth.

"Is he telling the truth?" Kalil spoke to the soldier who stepped up beside him.

"No, sir." The field commander was a veteran of many of Kalil's artifact raids; he knew what to look for. "We took in many notes, books, and excellent artifacts but none of my men saw any scrolls. Perhaps they are stored in some of these containers." He pointed to the blue and white fiberglass tubs being loaded into the smaller helicopter.

Kalil cursed and struck Toussaint's face with the pistol in frustration. He stood with his back to the Frenchman who was gasping for breath through bleeding lips.

"Damn Larson," Kalil muttered under his breath. He was afraid it might not be this easy. What if Larson was too clever to leave the precious scrolls here to be researched. He had probably taken them to Cairo to the meeting of his precious idiots, The Safari Adventure Company.

There was only one way to be sure. Kalil unsheathed a long chrome-bladed hunting knife. One edge was razor sharp and could slice the thinnest hair. The other side of the heavy blade was serrated for sawing and tearing the flesh of the toughest animal. Kalil turned it over slowly in Toussaint's face until the bright sun reflected into the man's bruised eye. Toussaint squinted in pain from the blinding light.

"Sir!" shouted the pilot of Kalil's helicopter. "The radar reports two incoming aircraft approaching fast. We must go."

"Tell me, Dr. Toussaint," said Kalil softly as he reached out to grab the ponytail at its base and jerk it back tightly, "is there a great future for a blind archaeologist?"

Toussaint tried to be brave but he was not a soldier trained for interrogation or battle. Tears ran from his eyes and he began to quietly beg Kalil to let him go. Kalil pulled Toussaint's head to one side and flipped the knife over to the jagged edge. He began sawing off Toussaint's ear at the base very slowly. Toussaint screamed at the burning pain.

"I saw everything on your little video show. I know they are here. All you have to do is tell me where the documents are and we will leave you alone," Kalil soothed in a rasping whisper.

"The tent!" Toussaint shouted.

"The green tent! There is a container marked First Aid in the green tent. Everything is packed in airtight compartments in there." Then he began to sob. His eyes begged wildly to be spared.

Kalil flicked the razor edge of the knife up with a quick jerk and neatly sliced off a small piece of the top of Toussaint's ear. "Oops!" He apologized and laughed. "I really should avoid the career of a barber!" The soldier laughed along with his cruel boss. Then they ran to the green tent and brought out the aluminum container with First Aid stenciled in bright red letters.

With one foot on the step of the black unmarked helicopter, he signaled for the soldiers to lift off. Toussaint watched as the chopper stopped and hovered just fifty yards away from shore. He thought he heard Kalil shouting at Sara over the clattering helicopter engine. He watched in horror as they tossed her out the door, screaming until she disappeared into the waves of the sea. The aircraft lifted off a few feet, then suddenly evaporated in a turbine whoosh over the horizon.

The Island

This is way, way, way too low to be going this fast! Jim thought. Larson was at full throttle on the helicopter. The cresting waves beneath them sped by like sand dunes. They were racing across the Mediterranean heading almost due north toward Greece.

"How are you doing?" Larson spoke over his radio headset.

Jim gave a thumbs up.

"I gotta hand it to ya. I love your determination," said Larson. "I am glad you are along." He scanned the instrument panel and made a few slight adjustments to the controls. "Nearly there," he announced without looking up. "I am almost afraid to see…"

Jim nodded and returned his gaze to the landscape. Was it possible that after experiencing the loss of his friend Weinberg once in the African bush only to learn he had survived, he would travel all the way to Egypt only to have him die practically before his very eyes? Jim thought of the video they had watched and the shot of Weinberg waving from the caves. The purple scar was there because he had offered his life to an attacking panther to save Jim. If Weinberg were still alive, Jim would do all he could to save him this time.

The island appeared in the distance as a white blur in the sea. As they approached it began to take shape in the form of a rough hill sticking out of the Mediterranean. Patches of sandy beaches lined with scattered short windblown trees alternated with rocky coastlines that shot up to cliffs high above the water. Across the top, they could see a small town spread out on the highest points, with zigzags of land containing houses and little scraps of tillable soil farther away from the top. Neatly landscaped green grass and trees capped by white stucco houses in the Greek architecture style dotted the coastline as they approached from the South.

Larson banked the helicopter hard to the right to circle to the East. Jim grabbed the seat and looked to his right. He was flying sideways and it scared him to think what might happen if they dipped down a few feet.

"I have no intention of being seen if I can avoid it, so I am coming in low and fast."

"Cool," said Jim, but he didn't mean it.

"Here we go." Larson announced as he pulled the chopper up and over a ridge, jamming Jim's stomach into his throat and forcing him to grip the metal seat frame in panic. They were the first outsiders to reach the scene. They could see someone had gotten loose of the plastic handcuff wraps and was setting the others free. Two of the men had already run to their fallen friends and knelt weeping at their sides.

As the chopper set down in the tracks where the commandos had just left, Larson sprang out of it instantly, not waiting for the blades to slow. The archaeologists and workers nearby ran to him and began shouting all at once.

Behind them approaching from the sea were two other helicopters closing fast for a landing. Each had the same markings as the one he'd flown in on. Jim wondered how big and connected the Safari Adventure Company might actually be.

Larson, a veteran and talented leader, began barking out orders. People responded at once and, in moments, everything that needed to happen had begun. The staff people were on the radio contacting predetermined military contacts to intercept Kalil, if possible, and to get rescue medical help on the way.

Finding out where Toussaint was, Larson hurried to his side. Jim followed closely, trying not to stare at the bodies downed forever. The two men ran toward the archaeology area through overturned tables, benches, and shattered clay pots.

Jim surveyed the surroundings and tried to look toward the direction he had seen Weinberg. Disoriented, he searched the surrounding hills for the cave he knew was there.

"Larson!" the unmistakable French accent came from the main tent.

"Toussaint!" Larson sprinted to the tent and arrived first. He tore into the fabric until he reached his friend.

"Easy, guy, It's okay now," said Larson as he refused to let Toussaint stand up. Toussaint's face was covered with blood. "Jim, hurry and get the medical kit!"

Jim turned and disappeared out of the tent. The paramedic-trained members of the team arrived shortly. As they bandaged his ear and gave Toussaint a painkiller shot, Larson debriefed him about the raid.

"Damn." Larson mumbled. "I cannot believe even Kalil would do something this crazy. He is out of control."

"Larson, he took Sara, but then…" his voiced caught in his throat. "Then he tossed her off the helicopter into the sea out there." He pointed off shore. "And, my friend, there is one thing more. I want you to know, I gave him the medical kit with the scrolls inside."

"Toussaint, it's okay. You did what you had to do. I am just glad to find you alive, my friend," Larson said.

"Where is Weinberg?" Jim finally got to ask Toussaint. "Everyone is accounted for but him."

"Oh my goodness. That is right." Toussaint tried to sit up as if to go search. "Where *is* Weinberg? He was coming down the hill from the cave when this madness all began."

"Weinberg is a crafty old fox. We saw him on the video way over there," Larson pointed inland to the trees at the back of the beach.

"If he is not here, then Larson, you know already where he will be found. Let's go there now and see."

"I don't think so Toussaint. You'd better stay here. Jim, you…"

"Coming," interrupted Jim.

"I will not stay here while you two go find him!" Toussaint rolled on his side and tried to get to his feet. "Of course you wouldn't, old friend," Larson said, giving him a hand to get up. "Come on, we'll go together. But first, we must do our best to find Sara."

Jim reached around to steady Toussaint, who, once on his feet, needed no further assistance. He dusted himself off, stretched with his arms over his head, winced, and drew two deep breaths through his nose. "Let's see now. I am missing something, am I not?"

"Here," Larson handed him a pair of wire-rimmed glasses. Toussaint put them on his nose and stretched the earpieces behind each ear. They were badly bent on one side and sat crooked on his face. Toussaint screwed up his face as his eyes adjusted. Jim and Larson could barely stifle a laugh.

"Ahhh…watch this – this is not a problem at all." Toussaint bent the side frame to the position he wanted and it magically stayed put. He popped them back on his bruised face and announced, "Gentlemen, shall we proceed?"

The three men turned and hurried around the perimeter of the camp and down to the beach. As they left the site behind, Toussaint said, "Before I came to this island, I did not know any of these people. But in the last few weeks, we worked very hard, side-by-side. I knew them well. The men who died both have families, Larson." His voice caught...he put his hand to his face.

When they reached the crest of the hill, they all turned to look back. The sleek helicopter seemed to be keeping a silent vigil on the death and stillness that lay around it.

"I made my mind up a long time ago that I would give my life to bring the Library we seek safely intact for the world to study and see. And I would not sacrifice the importance of that goal for my personal revenge. But I swear, I hope I get the chance to extract the price of this horror from Kalil while I am yet alive."

Larson put his hand on his friend's shoulder. They had both been through more grief this day than Jim had experience in his entire life.

"This I swear. This...I swear," Toussaint finished. He stepped up to the edge of the water and cupped his hand over his eyes to block the sun. Jim turned to scan the water for a sign of the woman he'd only seen on the video. Out of the corner of his eye, he saw Toussaint feint and fall backward onto the beach.

Larson and Jim dragged Toussaint off the shore. Soon, three Safari Adventure Company helicopters and two speedboats, each with a pair of divers in wet suits, were combing the waters searching for Dr. Sara Einstein.

It's A Fake

"Where *is* the Library, then?" A ten-foot-tall face filled the screen in Kalil's multi-media communications center. Buried deep below the surface level of his palatial home, the center boasted over ten million dollars worth of high tech electronics. For surveillance, he could watch digs and antiquities operations all around the world. He had enlisted the paid assistance of some of the world's top covert operatives and could send and receive heavily cloaked communications with his elite clientele in comfortable secrecy.

But, even for Kalil, this was an extraordinary customer. The client was by far the most important, the wealthiest, and the most ruthless one he'd ever known. Working with the eccentric and powerful German was a dangerous game Kalil loved.

"Our people are working night and day to translate the manuscripts, Herr Kreullar," Kalil answered evenly, using the word Herr in an obvious attempt at pleasing the ego of his severe client. "As soon as we have a clear picture of how to proceed, you will be notified immediately and a top level team dispatched to the area."

"Of course, I will be happy to volunteer my special security force to assist you, Kalil." The face on the screen was proud and handsome. A square jaw swept up to high cheekbones and pale blue eyes, a shock of blond hair so light it was a cross between golden straw and white ice in the light of the camera. An expensive black suit with a conservative dark red tie filled in below the chin.

"That will not be necessary, thank you," said Kalil, smiling to contain his irritation with the aggressive German. "We have a full complement of the best-trained professionals and a detailed plan of action. Nothing is left to chance."

"When do you suppose your translators will have deciphered the location of the Library, then?" Kreullar persisted. "I have some very important plans and a critical time table to keep."

"These things take time, Herr Kreullar. It is not like translating a letter from French to, say, German. These fragments are two thousand years old, written on goatskins and papyrus parchment. They are fragile and crumble at the slightest touch. If we do not carefully prepare them, these little bits of crumbs, they can be jumbled like much of the Dead Sea scrolls and take years to reassemble. First comes preparation, then translation is possible.

"Well, Kalil, you are the expert," Kruellar said. "You have produced a number of wonderful pieces for my friends and me in the past.

Kalil smiled back proudly on the two-way videophone.

"However…" Why did this irritating pest always end a compliment with a demand? "This is the most important project I have ever asked you to complete. Are you still so certain of success?"

"Yes. You know the complexity of our work on this project. Still, we are right on schedule."

"Two billion dollars is a very great deal of money, Kalil. Even a man as wealthy as you cannot imagine how much, shall we say, latitude that can give one in pursuit of his international goals."

"Indeed," Kalil agreed, greedily imagining the money.

"Well then, do what you must, Kalil, but remember, any errors on the acquisition of the Ancient Library will force me to take severe actions." The icy voice of the German spoke in even but persistent tones. "Very severe actions."

"We both seek the same outcome, Herr Kruellar. I will contact you as soon as we have any new developments.

"Danka. Good day, Kalil."

The German disappeared from the screen. It turned to a solid blue. A light on the control panel blinked twice and Kalil hit the switch for communication.

"What is it?" Kalil spoke into the microphone.

"Sir, the professor is here to see you."

"Send him in then."

The heavy walnut automatic door slid open silently on unseen tracks and revealed a short wiry thin man clutching an overflowing satchel of papers and files. In his early sixties by any reasonable guess, he was wearing a short-sleeved plaid cotton shirt and brown polyester slacks at least half his age. They were strapped around his skinny waistline by a thin cracked belt. One look at the professor and it was clear his priorities were not fashion but utility.

A shock of his white hair curled toward the sky and stopped for no reason on an otherwise bald head. Thin-wire rimmed oval spectacles bound his wide face, almost constantly in need of cleaning. Looking into the glasses on his pink whiskerless face, one would see a pair of inquisitive eyes; the eyes of a scientist were the eyes of a curious child.

Avi had been a scientist since he was four years old when his mother had discovered him conducting experiments with her cooking spices and dishes one morning. Within two days of getting his first chemistry set at age six, he had managed to blow a hole the size of a car in the wall of the shed at the back of the family home.

An award-winning student, he had completed high school and university far ahead of his peers and received his Ph.D. in archaeological science at age 24. He had labored for years in the academic world after losing his wife to leukemia soon after she bore him a beautiful daughter, he became receptive to the invitation of the well-dressed Arab who offered him an opportunity to work on rare antiquities. His salary was ten times what he earned as a professor. Avi gladly took the job.

Kalil had been careful to keep the exact nature of his illegal dealings far away from the good professor. Though he suspected the shady nature of his benefactor's business, Avi found it easy to hide in the laboratory and be content with the fascinating work. It also allowed him to provide very, very well for his daughter.

"Well, Avi, welcome old friend," said Kalil, smiling. He had found it best to treat the old man with gentle friendliness. Any aggressiveness almost always put the professor into a passive-aggressive mode that seemed to mysteriously delay any actions on time.

"I am well. How are you?" replied the professor cautiously, knowing in his heart that at best Kalil was a cut-throat business man, never his friend."

"What have the voices of the centuries said to you today?" Kalil continued.

Looking up from his smeared round spectacles, he stared right at Kalil. "Well, Kalil, the voices of the centuries are telling me that your research team made a big mistake."

"What do you mean?" Kalil sat up straight in his command center swivel chair.

"The documents you gave me were supposed to contain information about an inventory of artifacts, right? A collection of ancient books and such?"

"Yes, a sort of library. What have you found?" Kalil cut the friendly banter from his sentences.

"Well, I have good news and bad news."

"No riddles today, Avi. Please tell me what you have found."

"The good news is, the manuscripts you have found were in remarkably good condition. They were in such good shape that we were able to literally roll most of them out on the table and just start reading them. Of course, we photographed them and did all the proper preparation."

"Yes," interrupted Kalil impatiently. "What do they *say?*"

Avi began spreading out several photocopy sheets on the console in front of Kalil. "There are mostly business documents and legal transactions. One particularly good one recounts the case of a woman who was trying to get the judge to execute her husband. Seems he had been caught right in the middle of…"

"That is no concern of mine," Kalil threw up his hands. He had poured through piles of ancient transaction documents many times. Any written records of the past were the delight of archaeologists and others for the light they shed on daily life of the day. Now he was hunting for a much bigger prize.

Avi stepped back at the outburst of his boss. Kalil sensed the particular old man would shut down if he did not take care.

"I am sorry, old friend," he calmed down and smiled. "Please, tell me about the Library."

"There is no Library," Avi said flatly.

"No Library?"

"There are pages of business documents and letters but nothing even remotely resembling what you described to me." Avi pointed to a few documents and continued to explain, but Kalil's mind was racing in a dozen different directions. His spies had guaranteed the discovery before Larson had announced it to the Safari Adventure Company. If the documents were not there at the site, then where were they?"

"…Then there are letters from the man to his wife explaining why he had to remain in Egypt. It's a little like tapping in to a phone line only it's a two-thousand-year-old call. I suppose…"

"Thank you very much Avi, Please continue to record and document what you have. Now, I have a very important call to make if you will please excuse me." He rounded up the professor's papers and herded him toward the sliding door.

"Sir, do you know when my daughter will be returning from her assignment?" the professor asked as he crossed the threshold.

"Oh, I think she will be back here before you know it," said Kalil, offering his fake, heartless business smile. The walnut door clicked solidly in place. Kalil returned to the communications panel and hit a series of buttons. Static appeared on the main television screen on the bank of monitors that showed pictures from his warehouse to the cable network news to data screens of numbers that meant something to only him. He hit the mute button to dampen the annoying hiss until the picture began to come in.

The screen revealed two commando dressed soldiers standing beside a desert-camouflaged jeep. One of the men peered into a pair of binoculars.

"Can you hear me Unit 3?" Kalil called out.

Immediately the man without the binoculars turned toward the camera, his face looking into the screen as he responded. "Yes sir! Unit 3 here, sir."

"What is happening there? Has the Egyptian army arrived yet?"

"No, sir. But we have visitors."

"Who?"

"A dark green helicopter with The Safari Adventure Company on the side landed here about an hour ago."

"Impossible!" shouted Kalil. "How could anyone have survived the blast at the hotel?"

"Who were they? How many?"

"Look here, sir. I will show you." The soldier with the binoculars assisted the other in queuing up the videotape. It fed into Kalil's monitor instantly. On the screen he could see the chopper landing and the three men leaping out onto the site. Just as if he were there himself, the camera operator had thankfully begun to zoom his surveillance camera.

The first man was tall and athletic. He was wearing a baseball cap. The camera focused on him getting out of the helicopter. He moved quickly, pausing for a moment to identify each of the two bodies on the ground. Because the tall man's back was to the camera, Kalil was unable to see his face. Could it be him? The form and size were right, but, no, it couldn't be. He had to have been killed in the blast!

The man rose up from the last body and turned to survey the area with his hands on his hips. He looked around the hills and, as the camera focused tight, his expression came in clearly on Kalil's giant screen. The blond American with his rugged movie-star good looks stared directly into the camera as if he knew he was being filmed, jaw set tight and eyes piercing in a boil of anger.

"Larson! You bastard!" Kalil leapt from his chair as if to strangle him, forgetting he was not only watching from hundreds of miles away, but it was also hour-old videotape. He returned the camera to real time and the faces of Kalil's soldiers. "What do you want us to do, sir?" the binocular man asked. "We can easily destroy their helicopter and leave them stranded here." He patted a missile launcher in a rack on the back of the Jeep.

"What has happened since then? Where are they now?" Kalil raged.

"They surveyed the site for about a half an hour, then they hiked up into the mountains across to the West."

"Where is Dr. Einstein, then?"

"She came out of the water and began hiking up the mountain," reported the first soldier. "Larson and two other men headed up into the same direction later. We haven't seen them since."

"They must be going to retrieve the actual manuscripts. Follow them now!"

"Sir, we cannot drive the jeep up into the mountains. The trail is too narrow," protested the binocular soldier. "We have no provisions for a journey on foot."

"Listen to me very carefully. If you do not follow and secure the manuscripts the Safari Adventure Company is seeking, I will personally see that you pay dearly for your failure." Kalil spoke in angry but even tones. "Do you understand me?"

"Yes sir! We will do whatever is necessary. But how will we find them in the mountains where there is not trail?" asked the second soldier.

"You fool. Did you not activate the tracking device?"

"What tracking device?" the soldiers asked together.

Kalil screamed into the microphone, "The one we placed on the *girl!*"

A Visit To Sylvus's House

With the sea at their backs, they looked inland across a rocky meadow that led back into the island. Jim and Larson had been climbing up and away from the dig site for twenty minutes and Jim was sweating from the exertion. He felt the warmth of the sun on his back and turned to see if there was a view. No postcard or photograph would ever capture the perfect beauty of what he saw.

The rocky hillside angled down to the tiny beach and into the deep blue of the Mediterranean Sea. The sun was setting, casting hues from pink to blood red around a thunderhead of rain clouds rolling in from the West. As if ordered by a movie producer, several spikes of silver lightning ripped from the clouds, followed by deep rolling thunder. Several miles offshore, rain began to fall. The sun noticed the shower and lit it in a curtain of orange fire.

Jim reluctantly turned around to see where they were. It was the kind of spot someone might choose to build an expensive home. Apparently someone had. Looking more closely, he could make out hewn stone blocks and pieces of sculptured columns lying in the grass and tall weeds along with the scattered offspring of old-growth trees that had been planted in rows. The carved stones and broken columns were bathed in the pinkish light of the sunset behind him. Jim looked back at the gathering storm and breathed in the smell of rain.

"Here it is," said Larson.

"Here what is?" asked Jim, turning back.

"Do you remember the announcement at the hotel? The part about finding an inventory of the items stored in the Library?"

"Yes, of course. But I guess I thought it would be in some cave or something. How did an ancient document survive...out here?" Jim waved his arm toward the weeds and broken stones.

This is the site of the first-century home of Sylvus. He apparently brought the artifacts from around the Roman Empire and hid them here. He had a clever and elaborate secret room built beneath the visible part of the house. For its time, it was very advanced.

"Sort of a first-century panic room?"

"Exactly."

Jim turned and stared hard into the weeds and toppled stones. Piles of reddish earth indicated where the team had been excavating. Larson walked behind one mound of dirt and looked down, then promptly disappeared into the earth. Jim ran to where he had last seen him and discovered that Larson had leaped into a hole shaped like a grave, but about six feet wider.

"Here we go!"

Larson ducked his head and entered what looked like a hole in the hole. White Rabbit, here I come. Said Jim as he hopped down onto the soft earth trying to ask questions at the same time.

Once inside, he peeked his head into the hole where Larson had gone and let his eyes adjust to the light. The narrow tunnel led down at a gradual slope. Larson was just a few feet down the entrance, shining a battery-powered lantern he had found.

"Did you have that in your backpack all this time?" he called to Larson.

"No, there are several on that ledge right to your right. See?"

There were several shelves and lockers lined against the wall with supplies distributed across them. Jim grabbed a lantern and flipped the switch. The sudden flash of light blinded him because he was pointing it right at his face. AARRGH.

"Settle down," said Larson laughing. "Let's go."

A dozen steps more and the feeling under Jim's feet changed from soft earth, to something hard as concrete. The chamber widened as Larson raised his lantern high to reveal what seemed to be impossible. The dirt from overhead had been removed to form a sloping ceiling about six feet high, while the floor of the chamber was solid, hard, and clean. It looked to be white or beige at one time.

"Where are we? What is this?" asked Jim, dragging the toe of his boot across the floor.

"When the volcano erupted here nearly two thousand years ago, it pushed a wall of mud and sand along in front of the lava. It came over the hill we passed outside and landed here. Then the hot magma floated over the mud and formed an airtight chamber over the house."

"Over the house?"

"Yes, we are standing on the roof of Sylvus's house."

"You can't mean it," said Jim looking around in amazement.

"Over here is the staircase leading into the house. It's in amazingly perfect condition."

"Stairs...to the roof?"

"Yes, remember these people, like the Greek islanders today, use their roof a lot. There must have been furniture and tables up here then, but now we have to look inside the house for artifacts. When we came here originally we had a good idea of where the structure was, but not at all what we'd find inside."

"When we cleaned off this roof and found the stairs, we assumed we'd have to spend months clearing the lava and debris from the house."

"Well, did you?"

"Hardly. I have been on a lot of archaeological expeditions and spent a few years of my life sifting on sites with a light paint brush, as well as blasting with explosives, and breaking my back with a pick and shovel. But this was the easiest find I've ever seen. It was as if this place wanted to be found."

Larson walked to the far end of the structure and descended a staircase into the ancient villa. Jim was right behind him.

He was not prepared for what he saw next. All the pictures he'd seen of drawings of ancient life and the tidy displays in museums he'd seen were fun and fascinating, but the old merchant's house was the real thing. It looked as though the owner would be right back. Maybe the family had just walked down to the sea to welcome a boat from Ephesus. Jim marveled at the original furniture, oil lamps, and elaborate art and drawings on the walls bathed in the soft yellow glow of the their lanterns as they swept the sights searchlight style. Mosaic tiles, colorful as ever, adorned the floors and the large bath.

"This is like nothing I've ever seen before...how did this place survive?" asked Jim.

Larson was examining the floor heading toward the next stairway down. "We believe the mud and lava topping formed an airtight chamber that preserved everything you see...including the library below. "Come on, we are trying to find out if Weinberg is here."

Jim followed Larson down the steps and into another room full of what was once simply a furnished house and now a priceless glimpse of ancient life on the Mediterranean. Through it they found the entrance for the library. Suddenly a loud crash froze the two men in their steps. Both turned their flashlights toward the sound and stared in amazement at what the lights found. There stood Dr. Sara Einstein.

"Sara!" Larson shouted.

The image in front of them in no way resembled the sleek professor Jim had seen in the video. She was disheveled and dirty Her perfectly combed hair was a tangled mess. She appeared to be still wet from the sea and shivering in the cool dampness of the underground house.

"How in the world did you get here?" said Larson as he moved quickly to her side. "We searched for you by the beach and only just arrived here ourselves."

"I didn't know who was on the beach or who the helicopters were," she managed to say through trembling lips.

"They threw me off the helicopter and into the water, Larson. It scared me to death. I thought I was going to die."

"Jim, go back toward the entrance. Remember those foot lockers we saw on the right side? Open them up and find a couple of blankets and a first aid kit, would you?"

Jim shined his lantern back the way they'd come and soon arrived at the entrance. Opening the lockers, he soon found a couple of blankets, a towel, three bottles of water, and a tan canvas bag with first aid kit.

When he returned, Larson eased Sara down to sit on a stone ledge while Jim draped one of the blankets across her shoulders. "I, uh, I found these towels," he offered them to Sara. She looked up at Jim and, in the shadowy light of the lantern, he thought he saw a smile.

"Who is this, Larson?" she asked.

"He is a member of the company, and was at the hotel when we saw what happened to you here. He offered to come and help. I think he's nuts." Larson realized as he spoke that Sara had no idea about the explosion back at the hotel in Cairo. There would be time enough to tell her later, he thought.

"Larson's right," Sara said as she sized Jim up. "But then, Larson is almost always right. Almost."

"Here, let's have a look at your leg," said Larson, shining the lantern on the torn pants leg. There were bloodstains on the tattered shreds. She drew her leg back to protect it even before Larson reached his hand out to touch her.

"Okay, okay, I can see you've got a bad one there. Let me take a peek and see what we've got, okay?"

"All right, but be careful."

"Here, hold the lantern, would ya?" Larson handed the light to Jim and eased the torn pants leg open to see. "You've got a pretty bad cut here. We need to put a bandage on it, but I'm afraid I can't get to it through the small cut in the trouser leg."

"Well, do what you have to do. We need to get going in case those guys head back here," she said.

Larson placed his hands in the tear of the pants and tried to tear a bigger hole, but they would not give. "Wow, those are some tough pants."

"Hey, what do you expect. I'm a tough woman!"

Larson was sitting on his haunches so he dropped both knees to the ground to get a better balance, grabbed the pants, and really pulled. The fabric ripped hard and fast, tearing from the cuff all the way to her thigh with a huge ripping noise.

"Oops," said Larson.

"Nice work, Superman," said Sara, trying not to laugh.

"Well, okay, now we can get this bandaged." Larson reached into the medical kit and found what he needed and began to clean the long cut, and apply an antiseptic.

"OUCH!" Sara yelled.

"It's not too deep; not that bad actually, but I'm sure it stings a bit."

"Stings? It hurts like crazy. Can you be a bit gentler there, please?"

Larson complied, bandaged the wound, and wrapped her pants leg with a light wrap of gauze and tape on the outside.

"Let's see how you walk in that," Larson said.

"Okay, help me up, guys."

She reached her arms out to Larson and Jim, and they bent to help her up, each with an arm around her waist. She put a hand on each man's shoulder and gingerly they raised her up together. Sara put her weight on the leg slowly and took a few steps. She was able to walk stiff-legged and awkward.

She put her arms up, hands out, like she was sleep walking and said, "Hey, the attack of the Mummy!" Both Jim and Larson laughed, relieved that she was in good spirits despite her ordeal. "Yo-Mummy!" said Jim. "This is the perfect place for your mummy act, too since we are in this strange tomb-like place."

"Thanks for taking care of me. It is so good to see you guys. I didn't know what was going to happen to me. I thought they were going to kill me, then kidnap me, then kill me again."

"Tell me about what happened," Larson asked.

She related the events of the sudden attack right up to the helicopter lifting off.

"What happened on the helicopter?"

"He asked me a bunch of questions about the map and the artifacts. They asked if the Thermos had the real documents in it, and I told them it did." She lowered her eyes. "They spoke among themselves and the next thing I knew, I was being thrown from the helicopter into the water."

"Oh my gosh. That must have been terrifying?" said Jim.

"I landed okay, and when I came up I wasn't that far off shore. It took a while to swim back with the current carrying me way down the beach. I got up on the land; that's where I got this gash on the leg, on the rocks down the way. There is no good beach there at all.

"I crawled up on the shore and caught my breath. Then I headed here as fast as I could. I knew Weinberg would be up here, and I wanted to make sure he was okay and that we could get the artifacts out right away."

"Sara, you are very brave," said Larson. Jim nodded in agreement.

"Thank you." She looked down again.

Jim wondered if there was something romantic going on between them, but he could see no signs. As far as was visible, they were co-workers and nothing more. Jim marveled at that, since the two had so much in common and were both single.

"Okay, then, let's get moving and see if we can find our British buddy," said Larson.

The trio gathered what they could and moved down the passage, Sara walking stiffly behind Larson with the blanket still around her and Jim at the rear. Both men had lanterns held up for maximum brightness in the pitch-black darkness of the underground palace.

Around a sharp right turn, the hallway turned to the inside of the house. They entered a large main room and stopped to take in the impressive sight. Incredibly, it was about two stories high! Four delicately carved pillars spanned a huge fireplace still blackened from the blazes that must have provided heat and light to the owner centuries ago. Two mammoth lions, their mouths frozen in a vicious snarl for all time, guarded the entrance to a staircase that led up to an unseen level. Strange symbols and etched images from a time long forgotten adorned the panels on the walls. An alabaster fountain, mockingly dry, reached its mouth up to the darkness.

Jim shone his lantern on it and saw that two marble sculptured hands, clasped as if in prayer, were both at the center and top. "That must have been where the water came out," said Jim. Larson and Sara stepped up beside him, sensing his awe at the magnificence and rarity of the place.

"Walk around the side and shine your lantern up at the hands again," said Sara. She took Jim's arm and led him to his right.

"Here," she said pointing to the fountain top again. The beam of his lantern shone up at the hands. This time something in the hands caught the light and sent brilliant laser beams of sapphire blue in every direction. It bathed the room in startling color and beauty. Jim caught his breath in one short gasp and involuntarily stepped back to take it in. When he did, the light show stopped. He took aim carefully and, sure enough, the room exploded in a sapphire blue radiance once again. He kept his light steady and admired the sight.

"How...what is that in the hands?" asked Jim.

"We've had so much too look at here that we haven't been up there. Really without building in some kind of scaffolding or taking the fountain down, which we would never do, we can't get up there to see what it is," said Larson.

"What we DO know," added Sara, "is that the beams of light that come off of the jewel, or whatever it is in the hands, point around the room to several symbols." Jim followed first one, then another shaft of light to the walls around the great hall and saw clearly the shape of a symbol etched on the wall.

"We have just had so much to do here that we haven't taken the time to learn what it means. The letters are ancient Hebraic, we do know that," said Larson.

"As a language expert, I cannot wait to tear into this one. But even more as a mystery lover, I can hardly wait," said Sara smiling up at the sight, her face bathed in the deep blue wash of light.

Jim tore himself away from the fountain after the others had walked away to shine their lights back toward the fireplace.

Underneath the column on the far left single open door sat atop 12 short steps, worn smooth by the passing of many centuries of the footsteps of worshipers long turned to dust.

Jim ran ahead, his footsteps making a strange hollow thud in the empty stone chamber. He stepped up to the door warily, sensing the building would crumble if he were not careful to touch it gently. He placed his hands on the sides of the door and marveled at the coolness of the stone despite the desert heat. He sniffed the air.

"I smell mold." He wrinkled his nose. "How can rock in the desert smell like my old Aunt Marion's damp root cellar?" he asked.

"There's water down there, Jim." Larson stepped up to his side and past him. He switched a large portable light fixture just inside the door and handed it to Jim. The inside of the temple responded with a strange fluorescent glow. When the others came up to the spot, Larson lifted his lantern to reveal the hole that had been broken into the stone wall.

"When we first came here we overlooked this house completely. We figured anything significant probably was going to be found in the larger more beautiful temples back at the top of the valley," said Larson.

"Sometimes big things come in small packages," said Jim, expecting a laugh and getting nothing but blank stares.

"Weinberg got us to look here for the first time. We scoured the whole place. It's not very big, just a few rooms around the main one, and found nothing. Anything worth hauling off was long gone centuries before. We started to give up when Weinberg said he would like to do some ultrasonic testing to make sure the walls were solid."

"I thought he was nuts. As you can probably imagine, anything carved out of sheer rock has a pretty solid wall." Larson slapped the cool stone with his open palm, making a popping sound that echoed across the open temple room. "He found an echo here. Look carefully at these blocks of stone."

Jim rubbed his hand along the blocks and announced in surprise, "These are not blocks at all. They are only carved to look like that."

"Right!" Larson commended him. "When we began to look carefully we saw that they were carved up to here where there were real blocks covering an entrance. We broke through the wall and found..." he turned and held his lantern aloft to reveal a dark narrow staircase that led back up into the cliffs.

"Impossible," whispered Jim.

"Quite impossible!" The English accent was unmistakable. First a pool of yellow light floated up the staircase like a ghost, then Weinberg shuffled up the last few steps.

"Larson, Sara, it's so very good to see you here! You just wouldn't believe all that has happened," he began talking fast. "I ran back here when the attack began, and when no one came, I began to use Sara's translation key and you would not believe what I have discovered in Sylvus's scrolls! I mean…."

Weinberg stopped abruptly and looked at the other person in the group. He squinted his eyes, taking off his reading glasses for a better look at the face of the man who stood before him.

"My God, Jim! It's you!" Weinberg embraced him in a big hug. Jim put his arms around Weinberg and hugged him back.

He spoke too quietly for Sara or Larson to hear, but whispered in Weinberg's ear in a voice filled with emotion. "Man, I am so very, very sorry." He patted Weinberg's shoulders, sending little puffs of dust off the worn leather jacket. "I'm so sorry I left you…

Weinberg

He was in his late fifties and in exceptional physical condition, medium height with a soft charcoal gray to his once coal black hair. What most people noticed about Weinberg first were his eyes. They instantly knew they were with a man of great substance.

Larson put his hand on Weinberg's shoulder and pulled him close for a man hug. "It's just so good to see you, Weinberg. Thank God you are alive!"

"Yes, thank God," said Jim.

Jim had waited months for this moment. Sometimes it seemed like years since he had run away in terror after killing the panther that had had mauled Weinberg and, he thought, killed him while finding their way in the jungle. Even in the dim light he noticed the bright scar that ran along Weinberg's neck and down into his shirt.

"Jim, how on earth do you come to be here of all places?" Weinberg spoke softly. Jim stopped looking at the scar and immediately fastened on the magnetic eyes of the man who had opened his mind like no other. "I'd been told you were in Cairo but I never figured you'd make it here after the attack we had today! Welcome, welcome."

"I felt for your pulse. You weren't even breathing." Jim began and immediately the rehearsed words stuck in his throat.

Weinberg wrapped his arms around Jim and hugged him again, then gave him a brisk back slap as they parted. "Really, I…I…"

"You saved *my* life Jim!" *You* killed the panther, not me. You saved us both. I owe my life to your courage."

Jim was speechless. This was not at all the way he'd imagined.

"There is so much I want to ask you…and tell you, Weinberg."

"There will be an abundant amount of time to reminisce, sport," Weinberg said to Jim. We've bigger game afoot now. You are about to see something only three other people have laid eyes on in almost two thousand years! Follow me."

With that, he flipped on the bright electric lantern he was carrying and started back down the stairs.

They followed Weinberg down the narrow winding staircase in a practically vertical ascent. Gradually the staircase leveled out into a smooth rising stone path down a narrow passageway. "Is this the Ancient Library you were talking about?" Jim asked.

"Well, yes and no, Jim." Weinberg replied.

"What?"

"You will see in just a moment." He rounded the corner and disappeared. The group followed.

"Look up," said Weinberg. Everyone stopped and shone their lights up to the ceiling expecting to see nothing but a stone roof inches above their heads. Instead, they saw that the walls of the passageway tapered up sharply to a high cresting point above them.

"I think an underground river once ran through here," Said Weinberg.

"No way!" Jim shot back

"You are still a skeptic, I see, Jim," chuckled Weinberg

"He's starting already."

"Actually, the philosopher in him never rests." Larson smiled for the first time since the bombing.

"If you hang on a bit, I will show you a river that's still here." Weinberg winked and gave his signature thumbs up. A pile of rubble at the side was all that was left of the door they had broken through to get to the chamber.

"My guess is that these were here to ward off any superstitious visitors," said Weinberg as he entered through the doorway. The group followed him into the chamber. Weinberg instructed them to turn off their lanterns and switched on a light fixture along the wall. The room brightened with the same glow as the chamber they'd left behind.

Jim looked around and marveled. Stone shelves carved in the rock were filled with earthen jars arranged neatly in rows. Inscriptions on the shelf matched faded markings on each jar. A wide stone table sat in the middle of the room cluttered with the contents of one of the jars.

"Most of the manuscripts were in such excellent condition that we were able to pop them out of the jars and just roll them out on the table and read them. The conditions for preservation were perfect here,"

Larson said. He rolled out a papyrus manuscript scroll on the wide table.

"This *is* the Ancient Library! Its right here!" shouted Jim like a schoolboy who'd been asked if he wanted ice cream.

"Well, it used to be. Unfortunately, Jim, this is only where we found the manuscript that will lead us there. Most of these jars are empty. We kept the most important documents here just in case there was trouble. I never expected such a bold hijack but, all the same, I am glad we didn't lose them in the attack."

"What do you mean?" asked Jim. "The things that were stored here are gone?"

"I'm afraid so," Weinberg continued. "It seems that Sylvus managed to escape and get the artifacts out of this place. We have to study the notes he left behind to find out where he took them. Look what we've translated since you went to Cairo for the announcement," Weinberg said to Larson.

Although an experienced archaeologist, he was not an expert in languages. Larson stepped back so Sara could slip behind him around the table to the proper side for reading the handwritten notes beside scrolls. She pulled the extra lantern to the top to see more clearly. "This is too good to be true," she said.

"What does it say," asked Jim, trying to lean around the table in the small chamber.

"It's a letter written by Sylvus himself!" said Larson without taking his eyes off the notes.

"Well we don't have to go to a commercial," said Jim. "What does it say?"

"Okay, Jim, you've come this far," said Sara. "I will read the notes as best I can." She angled the light across the stone table and read the notes lying across the ancient manuscripts in the place where they lay hidden for centuries.

"Well, Weinberg, you rascal, you've done a pretty good job translating this for a rookie," she smiled.

"Well, your code breaker notes were great. I'm sure you will do a much better job," he said nodding his head in a jolly grin from the compliment.

Jim smiled. Weinberg was the most interesting and kind person he'd ever met. He was so wound up with excitement to be in this place, he couldn't stand still.

"Okay," Sara began, "I will attempt to read this right out."

She read very slowly, sometimes pausing for several seconds before blurting out the translated words, giving the whole recitation a nerve-wracking anticipation and delivery.

I Sylvus of Ephesus do write in my own hand, to you, my trusted servant Justinius, regarding the exact location of the library of God. After Santorini erupted I was able to escape by the underground river passage down to the sea. I returned many times to this room and took as many things as I could carry out of here to safety.

As you can see I have finally removed the last of the treasures and loaded them on the Blue Princess, my safest merchant ship. The journey will be difficult to the new hiding place. But I will guard these treasures with what is left of my life. They must not be lost.

The situation here is getting to be more dangerous each day. The fool of an emperor, and I know I could be beheaded for this statement alone, has declared Christianity an illegal religion and the soldiers are eagerly carrying out the destruction of us all. The decree is their license to rob us of our possessions and humiliate us in the most degrading manner.

It grieves me to watch as innocent people are taken prisoner and their homes, livestock, and children are taken as if the spoils of war for the good pleasure of the soldiers.

Though we meet in secret, I cannot help but feel that we will be revealed shortly. The priceless things of the apostles and the sacred possession of our Lord have done much to sustain our faith. Though I am besieged daily by those who have been misled into believing the possessions of the Lord and His apostles carry supernatural power. I dare not show them as I used to, to encourage the faithful in times of despair, for fear of losing them either in transport or seizure if we be raided as we study and worship, betrayed by a spy.

I am growing weary, in my old age. Perhaps this will be my final journey. I am traveling back to my father's land in Byzantium, to my home as a youth. I know you have never been to this place, but I have created a map and detailed instructions for you. The map is in the cylinder marked with the sign of "The Way."

If the Lord Jesus delays his return, and you receive word of my death, I beg you travel to this distant land and reclaim these holy treasures. I would that you restore them to the world when this Roman nightmare is passed. I place the highest trust in you, and also in your fine son, as one who has paid the price of the proof of his faith.

Sara stepped back from the table, still looking down at the scroll and gave a very unscientific, "Wow."

"Well, he mentioned a list of the inventory and here it is," said Weinberg. "I attempted to translate it but I am afraid I didn't get too far. These are not easy words."

"Let's see it then. Oh…" Larson let out a long breath, "there are even more artifacts and priceless documents then we had first imagined. This list is incredible."

"Yes, its unbelievable isn't it?" agreed Weinberg. "All the years since the last eyewitnesses of Jesus and the apostles died off, people have searched in vain for these treasures of faith," he said.

"In our lifetime, just one of these items, a scrap of an original autograph of any book of the Bible, or one of these other texts, would have been the crowning find of all of modern archaeology," Larson paused, "but this…this huge room filled with priceless manuscripts and the possibility of glimpsing…" his voice trailed off.

Jim looked from Larson to Weinberg, "Glimpsing what?"

"The face of Christ, Jimmy. The – face – of – Christ! The inventory specifically indicates several scrolls written in the personal hand of

Jesus himself. Absolutely nothing of its kind has ever even been reported to exist."

"But his face, Weinberg." Larson said again.

"Yes, there it is listed in the inventory. A painting of Emmanuel, God come in human flesh; a picture of Jesus himself."

"I have to see these things," said Jim. "What is next?"

"We must go now," said Larson, standing up suddenly and changing his tone. His face grew stern. "We have to get to the Library before someone else finds out."

"Sounds like a grand adventure to me!" said Weinberg.

"Yeah!" Jim added. "Let's go back to the chopper and go! How do you all go about such an excavation?"

"BACKS TO THE WALL! HANDS IN THE AIR, NOW!" a loud voice barked from the stairs they had just descended. Everyone turned in stunned disbelief as four fierce commandos moved into the light of the chamber. Each man was dressed in khaki military fatigues and clutching a rapid-fire sub machine pistol, cocked and ready. They switched off the battery-powered lights mounted on their hats.

"Your guns are set on fully automatic," warned Larson, backing to the wall and raising his hands like the others. "If you fire them in this chamber you could shoot yourselves in the ricochet," Larson's voice coaxed.

The last commando to enter the chamber spoke. "I appreciate your caution about the guns. Perhaps you would prefer to talk to my knife?" He brandished a long serrated blade with a cruel smile. "I will let you choose; sliced or shot? Now, if you will please step away from the table, we will collect these items and leave.

"Sure," said Weinberg. "After what you did back at the beach, you and your animals with machine guns, I'll just bet you will ask us to lie on the floor like a bank robbery and count to 100 before we can get up?" The veins were sticking out in Weinberg's face.

"Now my friend," the leader spoke to each of the men one by one. "This *is* going to happen. Right here and right now. You have no choice in the matter. However, you do get to choose how it goes. You can battle my men and myself, resulting in a certain and painful death. Or you can step away, let us have the items we have come for."

"You know we'll chase you," Larson said.

"Of course. That is why one of my men will be stationed at the mouth of the entrance to shoot anyone who comes out before twenty-four hours has elapsed. Now step away from the table."

Weinberg had slipped back against the wall slowly. While the commander spoke, he slid his boot behind the plug for the electric light that illuminated the room. In a swift motion, he kicked the plug out of the battery, plunging the room into blackness. Chaos broke out in the chamber. The sounds of screaming, shouting, and metal scraping across the stone floor accompanied the shoving and pushing as everyone in the room sought to attack their enemy and protect themselves in the darkness. A shot rang out. The explosion it created was deafening. A flash of light from the gun-barrel saw Weinberg clutching the documents from the table

One of the commandos switched on his headlight a moment later. They shoved Weinberg to the floor and the others away from the artifacts. They grabbed and loaded the manuscripts into ultra-light plastic containers. Hoisting the entire cache onto their backs, they secured each other's packs. The leader placed his thumb and index finger to the bill of his hat and thanked them.

"We do appreciate your hospitality," he said.

"You've seen too many Westerns," Larson said. "Is there anything else we can do for you?" he muttered under his breath.

"Oh, yes." The leader spoke as if almost forgetting something. In a lightning fast stroke he punched Larson in the side of the jaw, knocking him back to the wall of the chamber.

In a split second reaction, Jim crashed a lantern battery into the head of the nearest soldier. The sharp blow would have knocked an ordinary man out, but this was no ordinary man. He towered as big as a tank and barely moved, except to pull a hand to his head to feel for blood. He grabbed Jim's wrists and bent them back, forcing him to the floor. The leader kicked Larson back under the table in a one-two motion. Weinberg stepped toward him but was driven back by the knife of the leader.

"Careful. This has gone so well," the leader warned. The gorilla that'd been struck by Jim rubbed his head and glared. "Now remember, twenty four hours, look at your watch." Jim glanced down at this watch. It was almost eight P.M. "Anyone of you prairie dogs takes a peek out of this hole before then gets a bullet in the eye."

They watched helplessly as the men pushed Sara up the passageway. The light faded in the chamber until all that illuminated the place was the lantern on the now-empty table. Jim avoided the eyes of the others. The sound of footsteps up the passageway faded until their ears strained to hear nothing. Each sat quietly in thought for what seemed a long time when an ear splitting explosion blasted down from the entrance. Black smoke and rock fragments peppered the chamber at high speed. Jim threw his arms over his eyes and tried to burrow below the floor.

His mind flashed that in a stone chamber like this, he could be deafened by the blast forever. The pain in his ears would not subside, even when the noise of the explosion turned to the trickle of falling debris and the stirring of the other men.

"Who's not all right?" Weinberg's voice came through the solid darkness as Jim tried to open his eyes. He realized the lantern was out but relieved to find that he could still hear. Larson and Jim sounded off, "I'm okay," said Jim. "Yeah, me too." Other than the aching eardrums from the concussion, no one was injured. Larson flipped on his hand-lantern, its light bouncing off the walls of the chamber through the dusty air in a strobe light effect. They slowly attempted to either stand or at least drag themselves to where they could lean against the chamber's rough wall.

"Do you think they blew the mouth of the entrance up on the roof?" asked Jim.

"That's my guess," said Larson. "I was afraid that might be what they were up to, but I wasn't willing to get shot finding out."

"Shot in the eye!" Jim reminded him of the intensely vivid warning. "Anyway, if we were shot up there or in here a minute ago, we would have been spared starving or suffocating in this tomb." No one spoke, so Jim continued to project his fear.

"Admit it, the new guy is right for once," he said, slumping down against his backpack and flipping his light off. "We have succeeded in totally doing the opposite of what we set out to do." "And what was that?" Larson was shining his hand lantern toward the back of the chamber past the back ledge. The others turned to observe, but no one got up.

"We took ourselves permanently out of the race for the Library, and we gave the bad guys the map in one stupid move."

A loud scraping sound came from the direction of Weinberg. "Come here and give me a hand if you are done giving up," he said.

Jim stood right along side Weinberg who pointed at an unusual vertical outcropping of rock along the ledge. "Let's all pull on this as hard as we can and I will show you something amazing," he said without taking his eyes off the wall.

The men threw their weight into pulling. There was just enough room for them to each get their hands on it with Weinberg kneeling and the taller Jim and Larson standing up and reaching over them. Sweating and grunting, they pulled the hidden door open wide enough for them to slip one by one into a small opening inside the secret passageway.

A low mournful sound surprised the men.

"Sorry lads," said Weinberg puffing loudly.

"Weinberg," said Jim slowly suspecting something, "was that actually a fart?"

"Weinberg! Did you eat a skunk?" Larson said, bursting into laughter with Jim.

"Boys will be boys, I suppose," Weinberg began to laugh along with the men. "You wouldn't believe what they fed me back at the dig site."

"I already know more than I want to about that meal," said Jim, still laughing.

When the commotion died down they returned silently to the rock ledge, foisting their strength together along with a good solid grip. "One-two-three…" counted Weinberg. Then all three gave a hard pull. Remembering Weinberg's emission, they burst into laughter again. They sat down and laughed until the tears stopped. Finally they collected themselves and pulled the rock away, revealing a narrow passage out of the back.

They crawled one by one through the opening, then stood together and repeated the task from the other side, returning the hidden escape hatch to its original appearance with them on the other side.

Jim brushed his hands together and slapped them on his pants legs to get the rock fragments off. Larson took a quick inventory. "We've got water, some food, and everyone has a hand lantern still charged up. Correct?" They all answered in the affirmative.

"Larson, I am really sorry for what I said back there…" Jim began. "I am going to trust you to get us out of this and to go to the Library. You are a good leader."

The men shook hands. "Nice work cracking that guy's head with the lantern, Jim. He is going to remember that for a long time."

"Okay, you guys," Jim said to his companions, "where are we now?"

"We discovered this back passageway after we had been in here a while. We kept hearing water beyond this wall when we stopped to rest and it got quiet," said Larson. "It meanders down quite a bit more, then comes to an underground river. You won't believe where we exit."

Larson led the way as they filed one by one down the narrow way to the river. They made good progress but no one talked about Sara Einstein or the lost map.

The Reality of the Invisible

"Hear that?" Larson stopped suddenly and asked in a loud voice. The distant but definite sound of rushing water could be heard from way ahead of them.

"All right then, men. Let's get to it." Larson moved them on.

The passageway opened up higher and higher overhead as the sound of the water got louder. Jim occasionally shined his flashlight up into the cathedral ceiling so he could marvel at the purple and cinnamon colors of the different layers of rock. Inspecting the wall closer to him he saw a mossy growth clinging desperately to the wall in defiance of the impossible conditions.

Jim and Weinberg stepped up next to Larson who had paused to look down into a deep hole that opened up in the path. "Down there," he said, pointing his light into the hole. "Who's first?"

Jim reversed himself and began to lower his body into the hole, seeming to find a foothold just inside the lip of the hole, than another right away. It looked almost like he was descending a ladder. Weinberg wrinkled his face in doubt as he peered cautiously over the edge. He shined his hand lantern down into the hole, temporarily blinding Jim who momentarily looked up and squinted.

"Hey, Mr. Helper, could you please shine your light somewhere besides my face?" Jim said flatly and continued down the wall inside the hole. He disappeared into the opening. "I'm down," he announced back up to the others.

"Right then, I'm up," said Weinberg with a smile and a thumbs-up. He kneeled down and took an easier approach, slowly lowering himself down into the passageway with a serious look on his face.

"There are plenty of easy footholds on the face of the wall," called Jim from the darkness below.

"So there are," said Weinberg with obvious relief. Carefully feeling with his boot, he found many good footholds on the wall. The rope was barely necessary and Weinberg easily stepped down the wall backwards until his foot stood down on solid rock. Turning toward Jim, he raised his lantern and watched the soft golden light illuminate a long tunnel of rock, carved out by the relentless power of the movement of the underground river.

Jim took steps toward the water's edge as Larson plopped down behind him and began coiling up the rope.

"Careful, Jim. This wet floor is frightfully slippery!" warned Weinberg who had followed along.

"Isn't this amazing?" asked Jim of no one.

"Yes, yes indeed," Weinberg answered.

"A fine place to make a rest stop." Larson's voice echoed through the cavern. The men dropped their packs and found a dry place to sit on a wide ledge back from the sloshing of the water. Jim rummaged around in the backpack and found an assortment of nutritional snack bars. He unwrapped and ate two of them, chasing the sawdust-fruit taste down with a liberal amount of water from his canteen.

Leaning back on his pack then gradually slumping down until the pack became a pillow, Jim drifted off to sleep, grateful for the rest. Pictures of the last twenty-four hours rolled across his mind's eye. When had he last slept? He remembered waking up at the hotel in Egypt, the seminar with his friends, the bomb, the helicopter, and the island. He replayed the scene in the stone chamber where they read about the Ancient Library until he was dreaming it.

The next thing he knew was an explosion of bright light and loud laughter. Jim propped himself up on one elbow and realized that the bright light was the sun. They had camped right by the mouth of the cave but Jim didn't realize it because it was dark outside. He'd lost complete track of time inside the blackness of the cave.

The laughter came from Larson. He was reeling from one of Weinberg's stories out in the sunshine beyond the mouth of the cave.

"Stop! Stop!" he shouted, holding his sides in agony.

"Okay, okay, two frogs walk into a bar..." Weinberg began a new one.

"No please wait. I can't breathe!" pleaded Larson.

Jim walked along the river to the entrance of the cave. He emerged with his pack and looked up at the bluest sky he'd ever seen. Not a single cloud interrupted the Mediterranean postcard view. The river rolled out into a perfect oasis. A tiny, impossible island of tall swaying palms, date trees, and flowers on a carpet of green fanned out from the rocky cave. In the center of the oasis was a pool of clear water. Jim knelt along the edge and cupped several handfuls onto his face to wash the sleep away. He drank deeply then walked over to the others, running the last drops of water off his face and through his hair with his fingers.

"Sleep well, Jimmy?" asked Weinberg in his happy melodic British accent.

"What a wake-up surprise, though. I thought I was tucked miles away in the bowels of the earth, and yet I wake up here."

They laughed at his choice of words.

"I hate that you guys are always tricking me," Jim half-smiled in protest.

"We're not so much tricking you, Jim. It's just that you are out of your element. Everything comes as a surprise when you don't have your bearings," Larson said.

"Here, Jim, have some coffee." Weinberg pointed to the little pot on the portable cook-stove.

"Coffee? Who was carrying all this stuff?" asked Jim as he surveyed the amazingly complete campsite.

"See what I mean about being surprised by what you do not know?" said Larson. The others laughed as Jim brushed the cobwebs of sleep away with his first sip of the piping hot, strong but tasty coffee. It tasted far too good to be your typical brew.

"Weinberg, is this your...?" Jim began, suspecting the British coffee connoisseur of somehow bringing along his special exotic blend.

Weinberg nodded with a grin. "Don't leave the cave without it!" he boasted. "Life's short, at least the coffee ought to be good!"

The men laughed and settled back against their packs.

"Shouldn't we be heading out of here?" asked Jim. "Seems to me we've got a long walk ahead of us, huh?"

"Our ride should be here shortly," said Larson.

"Ride?"

"Relax, Jim. Larson's got things under control. This is a good time to catch up. It's been a while since I've seen you," Weinberg said.

"Well, I didn't exactly leave you in the best of circumstances. It's going to be a while before I stop thinking about that every ten minutes. Especially now that I am here with you."

"Let it go, Jim," said Weinberg, his eyes meeting Jim's. He smiled warmly and placed his hand on Jim's shoulder. "You did what any reasonable person would have done in that situation," Weinberg said. "Let's talk about how things are going with you."

Jim told Weinberg about his struggle at home with his wife and not wanting to go back to a normal job. He recounted his visits to various churches seeking answers and finding only social conflict. Once he began, he could not stop. The men listened carefully without interrupting as Jim admitted his desire to see the artifacts in the Ancient Library as a way of proving the faith that Weinberg had shared.

"There is another way, Jim," Weinberg spoke. The other men were tuned in to Weinberg immediately. It was obvious they respected him a lot.

"What you are trying to do, prove your suspicions of faith in the Bible and God, is a natural thing. In fact, you are a practical man seeking a practical solution and that is very…well…practical."

Larson smiled along with Jim.

"Every one of us, at first, sought the same kind of reinforcement for our belief," said Larson. "And there's nothing wrong with being aware of the reality of your faith."

"So," Jim began, "if this is the natural way we think and react, why didn't God make it more accessible? I mean, why isn't there something real in the world that we can touch and feel that would settle things. Why is Christianity hidden in the pages of this book in studying the actions and words of Jesus and not more obvious?"

"Okay, if you were God, how would you communicate to mankind?"

Jim thought for a moment, wanting to sound clever. "That's a very good question," he said. "You are the master at asking questions like this, Weinberg!" He stole a glance at Larson who raised his eyebrows and nodded in agreement. He had obviously been the benefactor of Weinberg's teaching.

Jim thought for a moment. "Well, I would…I would perhaps write the truth in the sky, big bold letters, you know. Of course they would be readable in all languages. Then I'd put them in geo-synchronous orbit around the planet so everyone everywhere could just look up and know. It would be that obvious."

"Go on," said Weinberg, "you are on a roll."

74

"Alright then, God, since he's God, could put up a gigantic thing for everyone to see."

"A gigantic thing?"

"Yeah, like that shape in the movie 2001: A Space Odyssey, that giant obelisk, black and smooth and totally unlike anything man had ever seen or created."

Jim looked at Weinberg who just nodded.

"Then God could put these things all over the planet, you know, at strategic places, so everyone would eventually see one. Heck, he could put a recording in it to say what he wanted us to hear and tell us straight out."

"Well, Jim, based upon that approach, why doesn't God just put everything in our minds and just program us up front to be his subjects? That would save all the skywriting and recorded objects, wouldn't it?"

"Yes, that would certainly simplify the whole matter," said Jim, folding his arms in satisfaction.

"Jim, you have two children, right? A son and a daughter," Weinberg asked.

"Yes I do." His thoughts ran instantly to his fractured family back home.

"Do they love you?"

"Of course, sure they do."

"Why?"

"Why? Because I am their dad."

"Do all kids love their fathers?"

"No, I guess not, not really."

"Of course not. For a thousand reasons, some kids probably dislike their parents more than anyone else on earth. So why do your kids love you?"

"Because I provide for them. Because I have met their needs. Because they know me."

"Because you've loved them?" Weinberg suggested.

"Sure."

"But they are free not to love you, right?"

"Of course, their feelings for me are their business, really."

"You can force them to follow your rules or face consequences, right?"

"Sure I can, for a while, until they are old enough to choose. I mean I can't force them to love me."

"You could write it all over the walls, put in tape recordings, and ultimately get them brain-washed and forced into loving you."

"Maybe put up a big thing," added Larson.

"Not against their will," said Jim, already feeling the trap closing on his argument.

"Against their what?"

"Their free will. Okay, I get it."

"We have free will and God doesn't want robots. He seeks a relationship with us apart from the robots of nature. Nature obeys his commands directly. The weather, the elements, even the animals are robots, slaves to instinct and forced to obey his plan. God seeks a relationship with us like you have developed with your children. Real and honest and free based upon who He is and what He has done for us." Weinberg spoke directly now.

"But why is it so hard to see?"

"Is it?"

"Well, yes, buried in an old book of weird stories and complex theology no one seems to be able to agree on. What if someone is alone on a desert island, or a tribe deep in the jungle? If they don't get the Bible, if someone doesn't tell them, how are they to know the truth? It seems to me to be buried as deep as pirate treasure."

"In the Book of Romans, chapter 1, verse 20, the Apostle Paul says, 'Since the creation of the world, His invisible attributes, His eternal power and divine nature have been clearly seen, being understood through what has been made, so that man is without excuse."

Jim listened for Weinberg's interpretation.

"You say the truth is hard to see." Weinberg paused and lowered his voice. "I say, it's impossible to miss! Look around you, Jim."

Jim looked down to the sea - Weinberg continued, "Write it in the sky? Have you seen the stars and the planets? The sun? Explosions of lightning with the power to run our cities for days are released in an instant. Thunderstorms and rain that water the earth and return in a perfect circle? Birds in flight? It *is* written in the sky, Jim.

"The first step in faith is the simple recognition that God created all this to get your attention. It's a gigantic clue, for heaven's sake! So without a Bible, even a tribe in the jungle can see God's handiwork."

"Through what has been made, the Earth and nature," said Jim.

"Exactly!" said Weinberg. "We are responsible for the light He has shone upon us. Each individual stands alone, judged by our response to his revelation. Look at the list: Invisible attributes. Eternal power.

Divine nature. All clearly seen by the creation around us so we have no excuse for missing it."

"Build something impossible as a sign? From the microscope to the telescope to the tiny hand of a baby reaching for her mother, unique design is abundantly clear in every inch of reality and you want more?"

"Okay then."

"You said God could put special *things* in strategic places as clues...? Here's a special thing...me, and Larson, and millions of other believers, not just placed strategically around the planet in a static way. We are alive. We are better than a special thing in one place; we are in motion so that anyone could run into us. We've got the message imprinted into us, uniquely in countless lives, cultures, and social constructs. A living person is a lot better signpost than that thing in the 2001 movie."

"So, we all see these clues," said Jim, "But you are talking to me about theology and a gigantic Bible full of information. What goes in between these clues and that? Where is the link?"

"Good, very good, Jim," Weinberg continued. "The starting point is to recognize that there is a God. The response He wants is for us to seek to know more about Him. That's where the journey begins. He plants this thirst in our hearts for peace, but there is no peace in the world. Once we begin to seek to know more about Him, then the journey really begins.

"I am on that journey now," Jim agreed.

"Exactly. You are seeking like a big dog sniffing around for something you know is there. But just because it's not lying in your dish, you are skeptical. You demand proof! You are insisting that truth prove itself to you."

"So what is next? What should I do?"

"I think you ought to pay attention to the fact that you are first of all experiencing this seeking. Isn't it interesting this is happening? Aren't you curious about the nature of your own curiosity? If you consider the possibility that this intuition you are feeling so strongly could actually be supernatural...and not evolutionary, not mid-life crisis... maybe you can fine-tune your channel and pick up a clearer signal.

"Could you be more philosophically vague?"

"Probably, but remember, it's not easy trying to describe a color to you that as yet, you are not able to see."

The distant pulsing sound of a helicopter grew audible, blended with the sound of the desert wind.

"What you should do now is come with us to Jerusalem," Weinberg said seriously.

"A khaki and maroon helicopter with the words Safari Adventure Company stenciled on the side appeared and settled down in the sand nearby, creating a hurricane of stinging sand.

The Rabbi

The city of Jerusalem sat atop the highest point in the area and teemed with visitors and pilgrims from all corners of the planet. Jim and his companions walked a short distance from the Radisson Jerusalem Hotel to the ancient walled city. Centuries ago, the city had grown beyond the perimeter of the ancient walls and spilled out across the hillside. Generation after generation had built upon the one before it, creating a city upon many cities stretching back at least four thousand years to the time of King David and Solomon.

Jim entered through the "Sheep Gate" past the high stone walls of the old city just as millions had done for centuries. Giant blocks of gray stone made a castle wall effect on either side. Crowds filed through the narrow opening; avoiding stepping on the dozens of vendors sitting on the ground hawking everything from fruits and vegetables to cigarettes and every imaginable product in between. As they walked, Weinberg filled Jim in on the history of the place.

"This city really blows my mind," he said, admiring the walls around the gate as they approached it. "Built two thousand years before Christ, Solomon walked here, and Alexander The Great. Jesus himself walked right through this very entrance. Then all the men and women of history through the Crusades until now."

"Tell me what you know of Jerusalem, Weinberg."

"Now that might take a very long time," he laughed. But no one loved to talk about history or tell a story as much as the Englishman, so he began.

"Solomon built the massive Jewish temple, one of the Seven Wonders of the Ancient World. But though he started out with the God's gift of great wisdom, he lapsed into the Middle Eastern culture of having many wives and concubines and taxing the people heavily. When he died the kingdom began to come apart and a succession of northern and southern kings killed each other off in power struggles until the Babylonians eventually took the whole country captive.

"Go on, tell me more, said Jim as they jostled along a stone paved street smelling the delicious food cooking in the tiny restaurants.

"Alexander the Great conquered the area down to Egypt and over to India. When he died, one of his two generals took control of the land, feuding with the local Jewish population uprisings until the great Roman army took over."

"Jesus was born here during the Roman occupation, right?" asked Jim.

"Exactly!" Weinberg said. "And boy, did the Jews hate the emperor-worshipping Romans. They stirred up so much rebellion against emperor worship that the Romans finally gave in and allowed them to continue to have the only legal religion besides Roman Gods in their whole conquered territory. Under this occupation, the Jews believed the Messiah would be a military leader who would throw off the Roman rule. They read all the Old Testament passages to support this theory.

"In fact several men rose up at this time and claimed to be this messiah. But they all ended up being killed along with hundreds of their followers. People were very skeptical when Jesus appeared and reluctant to side up with him, especially when he did not demonstrate any military or political interest.

"Wow," Jim said.

Larson led them through a red doorway and into a tiny restaurant. The side wall of the long narrow room was lined with mirrors to give the impression of a bigger place, but there were no more than six small tables inside. The kitchen was clearly visible behind a chest high counter, the cook working away with a rhythm of familiarity.

"Larson, Weinberg!" shouted a man sitting at the back table piled high with papers and a calculator. "That's the owner and that table is his office," said Weinberg under his breath to Jim.

"Ben! You old rascal! So good to see you!" The men embraced and Weinberg introduced Jim.

"Sit down. Sit down. Hassim, please, some appetizers for our special guests." The cook appeared instantly with falaffel and humus. Ice-cold bottles of spring water sweating drops of perspiration on their plastic sides followed before they could even take their first bites.

"Delicious, as always, Ben," Larson said to the restaurant owner who stood by expectantly to hear how they liked the food. The others agreed heartily and dragged the flat bread through the creamy thick hummus until it was almost gone.

"More here, please, Hassim!" Ben shouted excitedly. Hassim responded with plates full of unidentified but delicious meats and vegetables.

After a lot of dining and laughter - only after the other patrons left - Ben stopped working and pulled up a chair. The tone changed completely as the men discussed the scrolls from the Ancient Library aw well as the events surrounding their escape and arrival in Jerusalem.

"Ben," said Larson, "we are racing the clock to find this treasure of antiquities. We cannot be sure who is watching us and seeking to take these things before we do, or to intercept and kill us to get them."

"Jerusalem is not a very good place to conduct business openly, but it is a fantastic place to hide my friends," Ben smiled. "The ancient city, as you have seen, is a maze that even people who have lived their entire lives here cannot unravel."

"But we know of no such place now," said Weinberg. "We need to hide somewhere while the translation is being done."

"Who are you going to use to translate?" asked Ben.

"Dr. Sol Ephraim," Weinberg whispered."

"Sol! He is a good friend and very welcome in your new residence, my friends!"

"What?" asked Weinberg.

"This way, my friends." Ben walked past them to the kitchen where a small door led down a winding flight of stone steps illuminated by a single light bulb in the ceiling. As they made their way down, Jim noticed how the walls changed construction material and texture many times. They were passing through who knows how many layers of old and perhaps even ancient construction.

The passageway leveled out quickly, ending at a wide metal door like the kind found in a warehouse. Ben pressed a button to the right of the door and waited. He turned and smiled. "Welcome to my home; you will be safe here."

Ben showed his guests around and made them welcome in his home. Jim marveled that the residence was so large, with so many rooms, since it was basically underground. "There is but one place to bathe," said Ben, "so I suggest you begin that process now." The men agreed and, starting with Weinberg, they took turns cleansing the dust, dirt, and sweat away.

Jim followed Larson. He peeled off the filthy clothing he'd been wearing and sat the robe Ben had provided him up on top of the sink where it wouldn't get splashed. He eased himself down into the hot bath and let out a long sigh of pleasure, feeling the delicious hot water envelope his skin. "Hot water – one of the few things in life that makes you feel so good and isn't fattening or illegal!" he thought.

When he emerged from the bath, Larson and Weinberg were seated in the wide living room area. Next to him was a stranger with a wild mane of white hair and beard. "Jim, come in, come in!" said Weinberg. "This is an old friend of the Safari Adventure Company. Jim, meet rabbi Dr. Sol Ephraim."

Sol stood slowly. He was a bear of a man well over six feet tall and husky like a football player. He extended his hand and Jim shook it firmly. Something playful and exciting sparkled in those eyes as they peered through the shock of snow-white hair. The combination of his size and his presence made Jim feel at once a little nervous and excited.

"Hello, Jim," he said in perfect British English with that unmistakably sonorous Middle Eastern accent. "So you have come to Jerusalem in search of proof for what you might believe?"

Jim was caught off guard by the direct question. He thought that people in this part of the world, unlike Americans, spent a lot of time with preliminary hospitality long before anything personal or business-specific was mentioned. "Well, I guess you could say that," he stammered.

Weinberg laughed. "Jim we had just been talking about you and how you jumped on the helicopter to help us out. I hope we haven't been too presumptuous in our introduction of you?"

"Well, I…"

"Please, accept my apologies if I spoke too boldly," said Sol, releasing Jim's hand. "But know this, young man. You are hardly the first pilgrim to enter the gates of Jerusalem on such a quest. I wish you all the very best in your journey, wherever it may lead you. And I offer myself as your assistant and guide if you should need such a one while you are here. I know the old town pretty well, and a bit of the history of the place."

"Yes, he knows a bit of the history of the place, he does," chuckled Weinberg. "You walk around Jerusalem with Sol for long and you begin to suspect it was he who built the place!"

"If a thing is important, then it bears paying attention," said Sol. "Speaking of important things, Ben mentioned he would be bringing dinner along soon." He patted his stomach. "If you are going to hide out in an underground bunker for several days then it behooves you to do so in the basement of one of the best restaurants in town!"

True to his word, Ben returned with bowls of steaming and delicious food. Jim was surprised at how hungry he had become since eating earlier. They ate, laughed and talked until Sol asked to see the scrolls. Ben led them down the hallway to a large room with several long tables. Bright lights burned overhead. Weinberg and Larson opened the container and handed it to the doctor of archaeology.

Sol made a long admiring sigh and gently retrieved the contents, spreading the document out on the table. He replaced his regular glasses with a pair of strong reading bifocals and examined the document for quite some time. No one spoke as he checked across the document several times. Without looking up, he finally spoke.

"This, my friends, is very, very interesting. But I know from experience that if I do not restrain myself, I will be here all night and I am very tired now. Let us begin again in the morning, shall we?"

The Three Ways Of Thinking

Rabbi Sol looked like a lizard. With his head raised a few inches above the manuscript he seemed to be crawling across the table, wide eyes looking over the top of his tiny bi-focal glasses.

Jim walked slowly into the chamber and plopped down on the tired brown overstuffed leather chair against the wall.

"And...?" Sol questioned.

"And what?" Jim said sarcastically without looking up.

"Your friends have abandoned you have they not?" The rabbi's gaze was again down on the table in front and underneath him.

Jim burned with frustration. Even Sol knew they had plotted to dump him! He still could not believe they were out on the trail and he was stuck here in this prison with this boring old geek.

"Yep. They caught the Katy and left me a mule to ride," he said under his breath.

"A mule?" said Sol. "What's that about a mule." Sol bent over the manuscript with a wide round magnifying glass again.

"Just an old song. A dumb old song about getting dumped," Jim said.

"Well, they dumped me too, James."

"You've got work to do. I am just sitting around here like gravel."

"Perhaps we'll join them later, eh?"

"What is that supposed to mean?"

"What part of perhaps we'll join them later is unclear to you?" asked the rabbi.

Jim folded his arms in irritation. He looked at him and already started to dislike this smart-alecky guy. The rabbi was wearing a cheap light blue dress shirt with a white t-shirt underneath. A collection of pens and pencils clung to his pocket protector. Cheap polyester slacks, light brown, and like the shirt, frayed around the edges. They were held up by a scuffed brown belt. Jim didn't bother to try to check out the shoes. In the U.S., this guy would be a mega-geek.

"Okay, then, why don't you learn something?" said the rabbi after a moment.

"How?"

"Read a book. Isn't that a good way to learn a thing?"

"I don't read Hebrew. Probably not any good reading in English here."

"You've got a Bible don't you?"

"Yeah, sure I do." Weinberg had left his Bible on the nightstand in the room. Jim had picked it up but was too mad to read it. He wanted to be on the adventure, taking action, not studying. He could do that anytime.

"Well, then. Read that."

"I don't really feel like it. Besides, I don't understand much of what I read anyway.

"How do you mean?"

"Well, I understand it on the story level. I mean I am bright enough to see that Moses threatened the Pharaoh, that Noah made an ark, that Solomon built a temple and all that."

"Yes, go on." Sol continued to look down at the manuscript.

"But when Weinberg or someone who really knows this book starts explaining it, they tie together different verses from other places, they read insights and metaphors into the stories or letters, and get a whole different meaning than the surface of it. How do they do that? How can *I* do that?

Sol smiled. "Weinberg tells me you don't believe what you read anyway."

"Yes I do!" said Jim. "Well, I kind of do."

"If it's a lie then why do you read it?"

"I don't think it's a lie," Jim protested.

"But what do you call something you only kinda' believe? A cartoon, a story or -how do you say - a whopper?"

"Why are you twisting my words around?"

"They are *your* words."

Jim sat there and steamed. He tried to decide which exit phrase to use to get out of the rabbi's presence without any more animosity. The rabbi dismounted the table, leaned back, and pushed his hands into his lower back, emitting a fearful cracking sound.

"Perhaps you need a key?"

"A key?" asked Jim.

"Yes!" exclaimed Sol, "a key to unlock the mystery of the scripture?"

"Jim thought for a moment. Yes. A key to unlock the mystery. Is there one, or are you just pulling my leg."

"As a matter of fact, I do have a key that works for me," said Sol as he straightened up and stretched his muscles. "I use it constantly not only to understand the Bible, but to bring clarity in all kinds of things."

"Okay, shoot," said Jim, standing.

Sol moved alongside him and opened the door toward the kitchen. "If you want this valuable treasure, you will have to make me some tea, Jim."

"Okay then." They both headed toward the kitchen. Soon the kettle was singing and two cups were prepared. Sol sipped the steaming liquid. "Ahh, I love the smell of hot tea. Don't you, Jim?"

"Yeah – yeah - sure do," said Jim quickly. "Now about this key?"

Sol began. "When you look at the world, you are looking through tinted glasses. Your perception of why things happen, what to expect in the future, and how the pieces of our lives fit together are preconceived. Their influence is based on our past experiences. This is a world view. You have your own unique world view, Jim."

"What, like Republican of Democrat?" he asked.

"Well, that becomes a part of it, but really I mean that all of your experiences and knowledge come together to form an expectation of reality. Knowing a bit of mine might be helpful in tracking yours.

"My parents were married very young. I grew up in a kibbutz in southern Israel. We were very poor but we had a lot of fun and laughter. Family and faith were everything. It was not until I left communal living and went out into the world that I began to understand not everyone was as fortunate as I was. Some had very strict parents who showed little affection. Some had financial success and some did not. Some were beaten and some were orphaned.

"Each person sees or "views" the world based upon their personal experiences. A poor person thinks in terms of scarcity and is frugal with resources. A wealthy person sees abundance and can be wasteful or aggressive. Perhaps, because their basic needs were always met, they might have a better understanding of investing versus spending.

"A friend of mine had a very different life. His father left home when he was in first grade. His mother returned to her home in a fading coal-mining town in Indiana, near the Wabash River, where she struggled to care for two rowdy boys and put her life back into some sense. He grew up poor in a farming community with a tough stepfather. He attended a small high school with only nine students in his freshman class. He joined a rock and roll band and spent the next ten years traveling in a van full of long-haired rockers. You get the picture?"

"What a life! But, yeah, I guess I see what you are saying."

"The life experiences you had growing up as well as your culture, region, race, religion, and many other factors shape the way you see the world as an adult.

"Even if they are wrong.

"Even if they have ceased to serve us.

"Even if they are harming us, we cling to our preconceived ideas of the world because they are familiar. The way you and I look at the world is crucial to understanding our choices and perspective. But if we shift our view, we can radically expand the wisdom with which we are able to think, make decisions, even how our very lives works out. If our view is limited, our world is small. Like looking through a keyhole."

"Okay, I get the world view idea. Why are you telling me this?"

"Hang on. In the First Century, there were three dominant worldviews through which people comprehended their world. They were each built around a question.

"The Greeks comprehended their world by asking WHAT IS IT? In other words, they asked this question of everything they observed. They evaluated life and its components by trying to understand what it is made of. So, if a Porsche 944 pulled up, the Greeks would surround it and begin to analyze each component. Can you see them? Gathering up their robes as they determined the paint, the oil, gasoline and tires and what compounds made them up. "What is THAT?" they would ask, as they took samples for analysis. Their final summation would be: This is a compilation of all these chemicals and parts. That is what it is."

"Okay. That sounds reasonable to me," said Jim.

"The Romans, on the other hand, comprehended their world by asking HOW DOES IT WORK?" So, if a Porsche 944 pulled up here, the Romans would be busy examining the moving parts and spinning the wheels, the pistons, the gears. Finally they would come to an understanding of this thing by how it worked."

"So they were the original engineers, huh?" said Jim.

"Exactly," said the rabbi. "While the Greeks were gazing up at the stars and debating philosophy, science and the makeup of matter, the Romans were organizing armies that conquered the world. They were building roads and aqueducts and a mechanized army that would conquer all the land around the Mediterranean. It is interesting to think that because of their world views, these two cultures blended. While the whole first-century European, Middle Eastern and North African world was under the military control of Rome, the dominant language was Greek!"

"Well, that's very interesting," said Jim. "But what in the world does that have to do with understanding the Bible? I mean, the Romans and Greeks didn't even write it, did they?"

"Well, yes and no. The New Testament was written primarily in Greek, the Old Testament mostly in Hebrew. But, don't get ahead of me. The third world view of ancient Biblical times was Hebraic.

"He break what?"

"Hebrew, Jim."

"Oh."

"Okay, the Hebraic mind looked at the world by asking WHAT IS ITS FUNCTION? While the Greeks were measuring and examining the WHAT IS IT of our make-believe Porsche, the Romans were turning the engine over to examine piston movement and wheel base to see HOW IT WORKS. The Hebrew stood back looking for the bigger picture and asked, so, what does this thing *do*? What's it for? What is its purpose? Why does it exist and what is its function?

"Okay."

"Then the salesperson would step up and say, "You know, if you lift this thing here, and open the door, and sit here, put your hands and feet here, and turn this key, you can put it into gear and guess what…this baby will take you from Jerusalem to Tel Aviv in just a little over two hours!

Now the Hebrew smiles…now he understands and place this in his world when he can answer the question WHAT IS ITS FUNCTIN?"

"I am tracking with the idea, but still don't see how it helps with the Bible. What did you mean by Western man using a filter."

"Western civilization, European and American, is the product of classical Greek and Latin or Roman thought. In the first five hundred years, all learning was comprised of the writings of the Greeks and the Romans. The church - keeper of sacred texts and all books and learning through medieval times and the dark ages - protected the writings of Augustine, Plato, Homer, and all the others.

"All higher learning taught to the privileged class in the Middle Ages and Renaissance began with learning the languages of Greek and Latin. Americans are the product of this Greco-Roman mindset. Why, it wasn't until after thousands of years that the Vatican allowed the mass to be read in a language other than Latin."

"The Greek and Latin mindsets are the languages of science aren't they?"

"Yes, Astronomy, Biology, Physics. They are all couched in the mindset of Greco-Roman thinking and perspective."

"Well, that's good. Isn't it?"

"Of course it's been very good to the world. The scientific method has brought mankind out of the darkness in so many ways. It has cured diseases, solved problems and brought enlightenment about our world. Imagine, a petrie dish of bacteria sitting on the laboratory table in a research lab by an open window. A mold spore floats in and lands in the dish. A researcher observes the contamination but is curious and asks, "Hey, what *is* that?" He identifies it as a mold spore and he notices it kills off the bacteria rapidly. 'Oh goodness', the researcher says reaching for his microscope, *'HOW DOES THAT WORK?'* Soon, through the process of observation and repeated documentation, penicillin is discovered."

"Through the process of asking these two questions, right?"

"Yes!" the rabbi agreed.

"Well hot dog!" Jim beamed. "That's exactly what I want to apply to this book." Jim slapped his leg. "Finally someone is going to take this thing sensibly. There have to be lots of people just like me who just need the evidence laid out in order to become thinking Christians. Right?"

The rabbi sighed. "Yes there are, Jim."

"Why is that such a bad thing? Why is proof such a bad word! Why is it always faith, faith, faith? There are lots of things being uncovered with technology today. They found the Titanic, they dug up King Tut's tomb. If God cared enough about practical people, Greco-Roman Americans, then tell me why he didn't preserve this kind of everyday proof of the existence and accomplishments of Jesus, the apostles, and the prophets. Where is Noah's Ark? If a thing is true, it must be provable. What's wrong with that?"

"My American friend. The problem is that you are asking the wrong question. You are asking a Greco-Roman question of a Hebraic document."

"Go on," said Jim.

"The Bible was written from the Hebrew mindset. The description of this world, the biggest truths and greatest insights, even the historical parts, are all imparted from the functional sense. The human writer, even the first century Greek writers, were communicating Hebraic thought. The people through whom God's truth was revealed communicated through a filter that was unconcerned with the mechanics of science. The information is theological, and only comes together as a work on the nature of God, the nature of man, and his unique relationship with God."

"Alright, I need an example then."

"I thought you'd never ask," said the rabbi. "Okay, Jim, what's the first verse in the Bible?"

"You mean the very first words? You mean in the Old Testament."

"As a Jew first, I am amused by that term. But for you, yes, Genesis Chapter 1:1."

"Got it. Jim cleared his throat. "In the beginning God created the heavens and the earth. The big bang!"

"Good job. Let's just apply the three ways of thinking to this statement."

"Okay."

"One of the hottest debates among scientists today is the search for the origin of the cosmos, right?"

"Sure, looking for our origins is important to understanding how matter exists and what we can expect for the future. It's the key to the evolution of everything."

"The rabbi winced, "don't tell me you believe that monkeys turned into human beings, do you."

Jim remained silent but his look revealed his thoughts.

"I guess then, since the Earth is mostly water, we will all turn into dolphins with telepathic cell phones next?"

"Well, it could take millions and millions of years."

"Instead of millions and millions of years, why don't we just say once upon a time? It takes more pure faith to believe in evolution from a protein swamp than to believe in the creation."

"Okay so science has replaced religion," said Jim.

"Oh boy, we've got a ways to go here. We do at least agree that science is hot to discover the origin of the earth and all things. And that lots of money has been spent on everything from core samples to ocean dives to space exploration to put together a true picture of what happened. It's hard to believe that the first thing the Bible mentions about it is baseball."

"What?" Jim looked up, surprised.

"Sure, in the 'Big Inning'...?" The rabbi laughed loudly at his own joke. "Anyway, the Greeks and Romans and you look at this statement and say, what really happened here? Big bang, black hole or whatever. Swirling gasses, that's it, you have to love swirling gases and protein swamps. Everything they cannot explain winds back into some fantasy like that. Why doesn't a lumber truck swirl around and form a house?"

"Well, what happened is a good question to ask, isn't it?" said Jim.

"It is a superb question, Jim. It makes for a fascinating debate. And science will extrapolate observable data ad naseum and ad infinitum. Scientests write papers and books about their theories. There's just one problem – no eyewitnesses – except one!

"And the eyewitness said, 'In the beginning I created the heaven and the earth.'"

"He just thought it up and did it," said Jim smiling. "I like that."

"The problem is, even should science one day determine the real answer, they won't get it by asking the Bible to explain it."

"Why?"

"Because Jim, the Hebrew mindset was unconcerned with your swirling gasses and atoms and black holes and such. What was the filter of the Hebrew mindset?"

"What is its function? What does it *do*?" said Jim, mocking the way the rabbi stretched out the word "do."

"We have a bingo! Correct!"

"Then, what is the function of this verse, Mr. Rabbi?"

"*Now* you are asking the right question, a question the Bible is prepared to answer sufficiently. The function is to explain the nature of God. And there is so much here. In one simple verse, we see that God is creative, that He made it all from A to Z. That it was an intentional primary action, not a secondary reaction to chaos, disorder, or accident. Throughout the first chapter of the Bible, we see God is systematic, organized, loves beauty, color, simplicity and variation, structure, order, and a little rest. We know from his actions and functional explanation that he created men and women as the final, distinct, crown of his creation, with free will and the ability to communicate with this all-powerful God in an absolutely perfect world."

Jim sat back in the old chair reeling with the power of the new way of thinking. He thought about God painting the landscape, the sky, the water with all the birds, fish, animals, and plants of the world. "Gosh, that's a lot!" was all he could say as he considered for the first time, and actual creation event and the Garden of Eden as a real place. He'd never for a moment believed that the story of Adam and Eve was about real people in a primeval antediluvian world. How could things have gone so wrong?

"But, is there no science…none…in the Bible? Was all Jim was able to ask, refusing to translate his external conversation to the new economy."

"Yes, it is there but you must understand it in its functional context."

"Give me an example of that, then."

"Okay, same verse." The rabbi rubbed his palms together anticipating the joy of what he knew would connect with his student. "Any good physics study must begin with the building blocks, the fundamentals. Genesis 1: 1 contains the first three factors of physics; the laws of thermodynamics."

"You mean time, energy, space, and matter."

"Yes indeed."

"In the beginning = time.

"…God created = energy and force…"

"And heaven and earth are…"

"Space and matter…" whispered Jim. A rush of thoughts washed him overboard. "That is just so weird…it's almost spooky," he shook his head.

"What is weird?"

"That the whole toolkit of the fabric of the universe - something that's taken centuries to even formulate - should be tucked so neatly into the first few words of the Bible and still describe the nature of God at the same time." Jim counted on his fingers as the Rabbi looked on curiously.

"Ten words Rabbi. Ten words that frame all of creation…"

"And introduce its Creator," the rabbi added gently. "So, when the Apostle Paul says in the New Testament, I still love that expression, that 'by faith you are saved,' Western man says, well, exactly how does that work?" Do I have to say certain words, or are there steps and does this faith come into me as matter or magnetic and can it drift away and, and, and…the apostle Paul says, 'What are you talking about?' He wasn't thinking of those kinds of things in the first place. The answer is just not there."

"I am starting to see what you are talking about."

"Tell me what you are thinking, Jim."

"If it is functional as you say, then it doesn't require the huge amount of research and sophistication of other complex ideas…"

"That's right. Go on."

"Then the truth of the Bible is accessible to everyone, in any language, at any time of the history of the world. Because it is about the function of life, it is translatable to human experience."

"Yes…Yes…YES! Instead of trying to figure out how Noah got all those animals in the Ark, we see God creating a perfect world in perfect love. Free will corrupted by Satan, operating on his own free will, to a temptation that turned to lies and sin. And God hated sin enough to deal with it in the harshest way, but also as one who loves enough to save, preserve, and protect the human race."

"Okay, there have to be more of these great examples. Give me another." Jim sat upright.

The rabbi paused and looked him straight in the eye. "For God so loved the world, that he gave his only begotten son, so that whosoever believeth in him shall not perish, but have everlasting life.

"Spend a little time on the function of that one. And while you are in there, see if there's not some physics and science, too?"

Jim was silent.

"Hey come on, Jim. Give me a hand here and earn your education."

"What?"

"We've got a manuscript to unravel. Come up here and help me hold these edges down and I will answer any questions I can."

Jim stepped up to the table and learned how the careful unwrapping was done. It wasn't long before the work was proceeding well when Jim brought the conversation back to what they had been discussing. "Rabbi…I was wondering…"

"Yes, Jim?"

"How *did* Noah get all the animals into that boat?"

Both men laughed.

Yad Vashem

"I am really starving." Jim announced.

He and the rabbi walked along the narrow streets, still inside the walls of the old city. A delicious dinner and a good night's sleep had followed a fascinating time helping the rabbi. They had stayed up late talking. The rabbi had shown a tremendous willingness to answer Jim's endless questions. He was beginning to like the strange old professor.

"Very well, then, let's step in here." They entered a tiny doorway into an impossibly small coffee house. The sign announced several kinds of espresso and sandwiches. "This should work for your Yankee palate, Jim. No?"

"Hey, now we're talking! This is as close to Starbucks as it gets." Jim smiled and licked his lips from the coffee aroma, anticipating the taste of the fresh brew.

"Yes, I have heard of your Starbucks. As if Americans think they just now discovered the espresso machine."

The owner forced loud whooshing sounds as he steamed the milk for a latte from an ornately detailed and highly polished machine of brass and silver. The smell was enchanting.

"Starbuck's was never like this," thought Jim as he added a little goat's milk to the strong brew he was served. The proprietor of the tiny shop, a young boy of about thirteen, offered a selection of pita-type sandwiches and pastries. Jim chose one of each, pulled his wallet from his pocket and paid the smiling entrepreneur. Once again he felt how odd it was to be in another country without anything but the clothes on your back and your wallet. His suitcase was now only a memory after the fire in Egypt. Still, he was having a great time.

Sol picked up two of bottles of water then they sat down at a small table on the sidewalk outside.

Jim suddenly realized he had been so caught up in himself that he had not noticed the rabbi had worn the clothing of the Orthodox Jew; black suit and wide hat. "Tell me again the name of the place where we are going today, Sol?" he asked.

"Yad Vashem."

"I have only known it as the Holocaust Museum. There are a few in the United States, but I am really looking forward to going to the one here. I'm told it is unforgettable."

"That is the reason it exists; for the remembering. There are people today who would like to revise history and make believe that Hitler did not exterminate six million Jews and tens of thousands of others in the camps. You've been here for a few days and seen a lot of the local museums; this should be a good addition to the things we've been discussing."

"How do you mean?"

"We'll talk about it after we leave the museum today, okay?"

"Sure, Sol. Then would you tell me what you have found in your translations?"

"The parchments are a treasure trove of information."

"You know what I am asking. Where is the Library?"

"Well, it is very sketchy still, lots of clues but no final location."

"For a scientist, you sure can be vague. You say, a little of this, a little of that... Is that how Jewish archaeologists always talk?"

"Some yes. Some no. I suppose," Sol chuckled.

"See! There you go. Vague Incorporated!"

"Tracing the location of something like this is a lot more like solving a mystery. As Indiana Jones says, X never marks the spot."

"Still, I'd love to know what you've found, Sol, what you believe to be true. You know I am dying of curiosity. Come on, will you tell me?"

Sol looked around as if he might be overheard, took a deep breath, and spoke. "It appears as though Sylvus escaped the secret room under his house and loaded everything on to a single ship and sailed to what was then Byzantium, now modern Turkey. He used his commercial connections to secure passage on a camel caravan to the Underground City of Kaymakli."

"An underground city... in Turkey?"

"Yes, it is fifteen kilometers North of Nevşehir, in the Kaymakli province. The modern city was built during the Ninth and Tenth centuries, during the period of the spreading of Christianity, as a city of defense and hiding sites. The eight floors of this underground city are built around a ventilation stack. The ceiling height of rooms on each floor, surrounding a ball, is two meters."

"Six-foot-high ceilings. I'd be taller than the roof," said Jim, measuring his height with his hand. "Hey, have you ever seen the movie Being John Malkovitch?"

"Bean what?" asked Sol

"Be-ing John Malkovitch? It's kind of a movie about a movie star."

"Malkovitch sounds Jewish?"

"Never mind, go on about this city," said Jim, smiling.

"Before all those hiding Christians, the pre-Hittites passed through there with their household goods and iron-age technology; They were a short stocky people and, in case of invasion or foreign campaign, they took the whole kit and caboodle underground with them."

"Really?" Jim was fascinated with the first-hand archaeologist tale, and even more so as he began to imagine he would go with the team to excavate the find of the century! "Tell me more."

"They actually built huge, immensely complex cities large enough to house 15,000 souls all dug like intricate termite holes. We know that they have eight levels of conference halls, kitchens, infirmaries, prisons, wells, air-ducts, waste disposal systems, food storage, wine presses, and wineries. But only four of those levels have been excavated. Based on my translation of Sylvus's writings, he arrived there to find only a few locals living in the level nearest the top. He secured the treasures of his collection deep in the lowest levels where it would be safe from the Romans."

"And this was a safe place? I thought the Romans conquered the entire area of Turkey. I mean it was practically in their back yard, right?

"Yes, the Romans eventually did dominate the region, but the underground city had a legacy of covert operation. Even back in the most ancient times, the inhabitants of the city would spend months below because of the elaborate tunnels, passages, air-ducts, endless wells to tap the underground rivers. Up above, foreign armies would poke through the rubble while the pre-Hittites would sit, snug as a bug in a rug, waiting for it all to happen."

"Well then, Sol, when do we leave?"

"I've already spoken with Weinberg about this last night. They are arranging the passage now. You just cannot swoop into Turkey in a helicopter."

Jim laughed at Sol's description. "I see your point, Sol. I guess you can't just rent a back-hoe and start excavating in a foreign country."

"Yes, exactly. They are making the arrangements for the travel as well as the supplies we will need. This will be a very unique situation. The city is definitely not a site for the claustrophobic. Remember, the original reason the pre-Hittites chose to construct this underground city was partially because of their limited height. And we will need to take warm clothes. Not only is it winter there; my resources tell me it can get extremely cold the more you descend through the tunnels."

Sol continued to speak, but most of it went unheard. Jim was already lost in a daydream, imagining the adventure ahead.

"I am finished if you are, Jim," Sol interrupted. "Shall we go?"

"Yes, I'm ready."

As soon as they rounded the corner, the sound of music hit them.

"You live, you learn, you laugh you learn, you love you learn, you cry you lea- - earn..." the female singer wailed over the crashing guitar and drums.

There was a full-scale rock and roll band set up on a small stage at the side of the bazaar and a large crowd had already gathered to listen. Jim stood with his mouth open and listened as they wrapped up the song and bowed to the enthusiastic applause of the listeners.

"They are good, aren't they?" a tall bald man wearing a ZZ Top T-shirt asked Jim.

"Yes, they are. That sounds like an American group; is it?"

"The original singer is Canadian, actually," he replied, "the group is Egyptian but they love Western music. They have some music of their own, too, but it helps pay the bills to be able to play covers of popular songs."

"You sure know a lot about their music," said Jim.

"I am their manager," he said proudly brandishing a neon yellow business card embossed with gold letters spelling out "Pharaoh's Secret."

"That's a really cool name for a band," said Jim admiring the card and   shaking the manager's hand as the band exploded into another song. "My name is Jim!" he shouted over the driving music.

"This is one of their original songs," the man leaned into Jim and called out.

After listening for a while, the chorus of the song kicked in. Catchy and melodic, it carried a beautiful mix of rock instruments and tasty eastern rhythm across the market. "I really like this!" Jim said, grinning at the proud manager.

"You should get the CD." The manager pointed to a table with their recordings.

During his Safari in Africa, Weinberg had encouraged him to be more in the moment. To drink in the power of your life by suspending the past and future so you could better sense your experience. For just a moment, he let himself remember to forget and merged with the day. He was trying to stop worrying and capture more of this special point in time of his life.

"Ah, to be in Israel!" he sighed aloud

Jim looked across the busy scene of shops, tents, and people dressed in so many different ways. The lyrical mood of the music blended tightly with the centuries-old market.

Jim bought a CD of the band. He slid the manager's business card in the cover. "Butts," he muttered the manager's name to himself, thinking he had heard it before.

"Sol, is Butts a Jewish surname?" He held the card out for the rabbi to see.

"Sounds German. Maybe it is a nickname, if you know what I mean," he laughed. "How would you like to have a name like that?"

"Yeah," said Jim, "ouch, huh?"

They continued to the gate of the old city and, in a few moments, were riding the bus to the Holocaust Museum. When they arrived, Sol paused to speak to the security attendant at the front and Jim entered alone. No matter whom he had been with, he would have experienced this place alone, he thought. No one spoke a word as they moved from room to room – stunned by the gripping reality of what they saw. How could this have happened? How could a human being treat another in this horrific way?

In their arrogance and pride, the Nazis had damned themselves into history by their own meticulous nature. They had recorded in painstaking detail the systematic steps taken to eradicate the Jews from the Earth while squeezing each ounce of value from them in every form imaginable. Unthinkable atrocities were leveled at the men, women, and worst of all little children in the name of maximizing the human resource from labor, possessions, and medical testing. They had finally even attempted to figure out a way to harvest the hides of the dead as if they were merely bison slaughtered on the American prairie.

Emotion bursting in his chest, heart beating fast, Jim moved into the last dimly lit room and froze in his tracks. There was no sign to explain this room's contents because one was not needed. There stood a silent testimony that seemed to Jim to represent the horror of what Hitler had called the Final Solution in a single haunting image.

The room was filled with shoes ... a small mountain of every size and shape, big and small, worn shoes. A used shoe has a whole different attitude than a new one. It is broken in, the laces are wrinkled, the bottoms are scuffed and the sides are worn.

This was no picture. You could reach out and touch them but you never would. The shoes of the captured, tortured, and murdered tens of thousands of human beings. Each one begat the thought of the foot that came out of it last, and what that foot felt next. And the thought of that foot led to the thought of the man, woman or child who had worn it, their eyes, what they thought and felt and saw as they removed their shoes - if they took them off themselves at all.

How could there be justice? thought Jim. How could a whole country have condoned or ignored this? How could a person who grew up in a home in the first part of the 20th century with a mom and dad and an ordinary life have meted out the cruelty it took to make this possible?

Then that Jim sensed someone standing next to him.

"The shoes. This room with the shoes, I swear it is many degrees colder in here then anywhere in Israel," said Rabbi Sol.

Jim looked up at him with tears in his eyes. He could not speak.

People moved through the museum in small groups or alone. They came from all over the world to this place of remembering. Some wept for relatives they never knew. A few relived a dimly remembered childhood when they survived the camps. But everyone was humbled by the shocking reality of it all.

Eventually they moved along through the exit and into the final display outside. There was a strange sense that this part of the museum was not yet complete. There were railroad tracks running away from the museum. Down at the end of the tracks a short stroll away sat a lone boxcar. As they approached the car, it dawned on Jim this was one of the exact cars that hundreds of people were forced into like cattle, far too many to survive the trip. They were hauled to places like Auschwitz, Dachau, and Buchenwald. He tried to stop his imagination from seeing the faces that might have squeezed into the tiny windows to get a breath of air, and what a German citizen might have seen in those eyes as that train rumbled through his village.

"Sol, as a Jew, what do you think about when you see this?"

Sol wiped his face with his handkerchief. "Jim, I lost many relatives in the camps and in the war. My family was wiped out the by the plundering of the Nazi army – and they never really recovered. It is easy to come to this place and think of the terrible things they experienced. You've seen the films. They can keep you up all night if you let them."

"I know," said Jim. "You told me that you would tie in our conversations to this place when we were done here. Do you feel like doing that still?"

"Yes, of course. I had not forgotten." The rabbi motioned for the door.

"The lesson is a simple one, so do not be disappointed."

"Okay."

"The function of this place for me is about one short but deadly word: Sin."

"Sin?"

"Yes. The main reason people reject a savior or salvation is that they don't think they need it. They have come to believe in their science, and their enlightened education, and circumstances. They refuse to believe they have a nature for sin, that they are born to evil intentions."

"Oh, Sol, babies aren't sinful. People learn to be bad and do bad things over time," said Jim. "It's the way of the world."

"Oh, is that right? Well then, tell me this. Do you have to teach a child to tell a first lie?"

"Uh…"

"No. You don't sit down and tell children that if they blame the missing cookies on aliens, wild dogs or their siblings, then they won't get into trouble. Deep inside, every human being has a natural bent toward bad things. To varying degrees, it is controlled by law, consequences, or learned values. But look at this place, Jim. Germans aren't bad people – not any more than anyone else. Germany produced music, wisdom, and some of the highest and noblest of human beauty."

"I never thought of it like that."

"A whole nation became a symbol for evil because they chose to follow an evil leader into creating the nightmare of mass murder. Hitler tapped into that part of our nature. Left to our own devices, we all - you, me, everyone you ever respected - have an inner nature that will do bad things."

"And...that means?"

"There are no bad things allowed in heaven." The rabbi gestured that they had talked enough for now. The two men headed for the exit. Even as Jim left the museum, he knew that the museum would never leave him.

Hide or Die!

Heading back toward the hotel, he noticed the bright sunshine beginning to fade into a blue gray. Perhaps Weinberg and Larson had returned. The bus wound through the streets up the incline to the gates of the old city.

Jim and Sol stepped down off the bus through the gates and entered the city walls. "Jim, I am going to go back to work on the manuscript."

"I understand, Sol. Thanks so much for taking the time with me today."

"You are quite welcome, Jim. I have enjoyed our time together. Will you join me back at our bunker?"

"No, I think I will stroll around the city some more and I will see you back there later."

"You have your own key, yes?"

Jim patted his pocket. "Yes I do. Thanks again."

"Jim, please be careful here. Keep your eyes and ears open. The crime rate is very low here compared to most American cities, but there is still the random terrorist element. God forbid, Kalil's thugs may still be looking for anyone who can lead them to the manuscript."

They shook hands and parted.

Jim strolled through the streets with the street map Sol had given him earlier. He decided to follow the famed twelve Stations of the Cross. Buying a map from a small souvenir shop, he worked his way around to the first location.

"Excuse me, sir." Jim turned around to see a bald, barrel-chested man wearing a suit. He had a wide bandage on the side of his head. The suit was expensive and tailored nicely, but did not hide the fact that this man was muscular and bulked up. Jim eyed him suspiciously. There was something oddly familiar about this guy.

"My boss would like a word with you," he swept his hand back toward the black Mercedes sedan with the door open. Jim glanced

103

inside. There was another large, and well dressed man in the back seat. "Come on, jump in, buddy," came an American-sounding voice.

"What is this about?" asked Jim.

"It will only take a moment, please get in."

Jim sensed the panic rising up inside him. In an instant, his mind tore through his options and, other than getting in the car, which he wasn't about to do, he only had one…run away as fast as he could! The big guy in the suit was just a few feet away from him. Their eyes met. In one of those slow-motion, frozen moments in time, the man took an aggressive step too close.

Jim took a step back and put his palms up. "Hey now. Let's just wait a minute here."

The suited gorilla shot at him with surprising speed and Jim dropped his map, turned, and ran back down the cobblestone street without noticing there was no one person in sight.

As he ran in panic, trying to remember the way back to the underground apartment, he flashed, should he even go there? Should he lead these men to the location of the manuscripts? He heard the sound of the musical group he had seen earlier blasting out a loud jam.

There were police and soldiers everywhere in Jerusalem. Maybe the men would not chase him into a crowded market place. He gambled on that hope.

Reaching the open square, he ran a few meters into the area of tables and paused. The band was roaring through a loud, fast, blues shuffle. Jim tried to get his thoughts in order. Who should he talk to? What would he say? What if no one speaks English? Every person was turned toward the music except one. His eyes found the band's manager, Butts.

He was bending over the tape table and taking some money for the purchase of a CD. Just then, he looked up and straight into Jim's wide eyes. His smile of recognition turned into a furrowed brow. He could clearly see the American he had just spoken to earlier was now in trouble.

In slow motion, Jim saw pieces of table and pottery shatter and fly all around him. The high-pitched crack of gunfire pierced the sound of the music. All the musicians stopped except the drummer, who could not hear the automatic weapons over his own explosions. The gunfire and the drumbeat blended into a bizarre rhythm.

Still not realizing what had happened, Jim turned to see the man in the suit and the man from the back seat firing at him. "This place is totally insane!" he thought. "They don't care who they kill!

The market erupted into a mad frenzy to escape. Hundreds of people rushed in every direction, shopkeepers diving behind stacks of rugs, musicians waving to the drummer who, head down, continued to bang and crash, adding to the din of terror.

Through the screams, drums, and guns, Jim ran toward an alley between the buildings. Along the twisted corridor, he leapt over boxes, trash, and refuse on the wet, smelly bricks and dirt of the narrow angling passage. He ran until his lungs stung for air.

Flattening himself against a shallow doorway, he tried to get his breath under control. His legs cramped and chest sharply cut from his exploding heart. The men had fired into a crowded marketplace. They must be terrorists. Maybe they wanted to kidnap an American. They clearly didn't care that they were seen by dozens of witnesses.

As he calmed his breathing, he listened. The alley was quiet except for the slow plop of water dripping on the pavement and echoing down. Then he heard the voices again.

"No sign of him yet. He's got to still be in this alley." Jim startled as he heard the American burglar's voice again. The sound of another tinny voice crackled an indecipherable message from a distant radio.

"Bring the car around to Havilah Street and wait for us there. I am going to shoot him just for making me run," spat the Middle Eastern voice angrily through labored breaths.

"You are such a colossal idiot," replied the American. "You already created a major disturbance at the market by shooting up the place. We'll have hell to pay explaining that to Kalil when it hits the television news. But that's not enough. Now you want to shoot the guy before he gets a chance to interrogate him. God, I hate working with you!"

"O.K. I'll just shoot him in the leg. It will make me feel better and I can say he was getting away and I had to do it," the rough voice spoke a new plan.

"You are such a loser," the American replied, disgusted.

Jim did not wait to hear any more. He furiously spun around with his face pressed tightly against the faded green door. The cracking paint chips dug into his cheek. He tried the door as slowly and quietly as he could. It would not open. He applied all the strength in his hands but to no avail. It was locked tight.

No time to think. Jim spun and bolted down the blind alley. The men spotted him and shouted as they picked up the chase again. He didn't see the large flat crate in time. It scraped his shinbone, tearing his pants and skin on the nail head as he tumbled face first onto the rotten debris on the floor of the alley. Sharp pain tore up his leg but he muffled a scream and scrambled to his feet. He had to keep running! Ahead, a shaft of light appeared. A street!

Somehow he found the energy to pick up the pace and raced toward the open area. Just as he turned to run to his left and through the short alley into the street, he saw two men dressed in dark suits and sunglasses getting out of another black sedan. They were carrying automatic weapons.

Jim skidded to a halt as they looked up and shouted, "Stop!"

Back into the alley, he continued on deeper into the maze. The closeness of the roof tops along the high walls blocked out the dwindling light of the setting sun as he ran along a section of mud brick wall with no door in sight. A wall loomed directly ahead blocking the alley. A sense of hopelessness began to overtake Jim. He reached the wall and turned to the right.

Stumbling to a dead stop, he looked up at yet a higher brick wall. This time he was trapped!

Spinning, he scanned the walls for any exit. The only opening was a steel door in the corner of the dead end. He began wringing the handle, scraping the rough metal against his palms. It, too, was locked tight. Jim attacked the door, pounding with his fists. No reply.

He looked around the dingy floor for a weapon, anything, but all he could find was an open box filled with bunches of bananas. He lay back against the bolted door and waited.

The two thugs came around the corner, cautiously and wide to the back, smiling.

"See, I told you this was a dead end," said the man with the bandage on his head. "Oh my God," thought Jim as he realized where he knew the man. It was the commando he had clobbered with the lantern back at the dig site. These men worked for Kalil, and worse yet, the big guy certainly wanted a shot at paying Jim back for whatever was underneath that bandage.

"Careful, he's got a banana!" said the American with mock seriousness.

The two men laughed as Jim threw it with all his might. They ducked and wheezed with laughter at the ridiculous sight, but the ripe banana landed squarely on the tie of the big man and exploded, leaving a wide yellow stain on his tie and jacket.

"This is where I shoot him. Watch," the middle-eastern man announced. "Stand still!" the thug commanded as he raised his gun toward the trembling Jim. "If you shiver and I miss my mark, it will only prolong your miserable death."

Jim closed his eyes while the faces of his family and a thousand childhood memories, raced across his mind. With shocking clarity he realized his life was flashing before him.

"Oh, please God, don't let me die!" he whispered, eyes squeezed tight.

"Lower your gun. You are not shooting anyone!" A loud and familiar voice echoed down the ally. "Throw those on the ground and put your hands on the wall, NOW!"

The band manager appeared around the corner with a pistol held tightly in his hands. He winked at Jim as he poked the gun in the ribs of the shooter.

"Oh, my God!" said Jim. "Oh...oh!"

"Are you OK?" he asked.

"What is going on?" shouted Jim in anger and frustration.

"I do not know, but I was not going to sit still and...."

His words were cut short. Butts stepped sideways with a frown, the barrel of a gun pressed into his temple from a man in a blue suit pushing him back. He grabbed the band manager's gun and twisted his arm around his back, forcing him face first into the wall. Producing a syringe from his pocket, he squirted a small stream, then plunged it into Butts's neck and pushed the plunger down.

"Do you have enough for the jack rabbit?" asked the big bandaged man, gesturing at Jim as he stooped to retrieve his gun.

"Sure I do," the blue suit said. He pulled the needle from the neck of the glazed eyed manager. "Got enough to stun a camel."

Already limp as a rag doll, the band manager slid sickeningly down the wall as the man turned and spoke to the Middle Easterner in the turban. "You have done enough damage today, you fool. Now, can you subdue the prey so I can inject him?"

"Sure. This will be fun."

Jim doubled his fists as the men stepped toward him.

In The Hall Of The Devil

The flickering light from the flame of a slender brass oil lamp bathed the room in orange shafts of light that pushed back the blackness of the tomb. In the center lay a large open sarcophagus. Soft singing in a strange language echoed down the hallway. Voices filled with sadness sang a low chant in a foreign tongue.

Jim approached the ornate coffin, marveling at the sharpness of the color and intricate detail of the painting. The museum collections he had seen were faded. This looked new.

Curious, he peered into the box at a freshly wrapped mummy. The bright white strips of cloth were wrapped carefully around the figure. A light-colored glue, still glistening and wet, seeped around the cloth. This body had just been prepared for burial.

The only thing visible on the figure was the eyes. The eyelids, painted a deep violet trimmed in black lines were closed naturally, as if in a peaceful sleep. Suddenly, the eyes opened and stared right at Jim. Piercing and wide, the onyx eyes of the mummy immediately flashed panic and fear.

And then…Jim was no longer looking down into the face; he was inside the wrappings and looking out! He tried to move his arms but they were tightly bound at his sides. He tried to move his legs but immediately felt the leather thong binding his ankles cut into his skin.

A scream of terror welled up in his mouth. But no sound would come from the lips held tightly from the cloth that ran over the head and clamping his jaw. The orange light faded as he grew hot from fighting the bindings. Then it was dark

Jim awoke from the dream into the terrible reality. He was bound hand and foot. He realized he had been blindfolded. He bit down against the rag they had stuffed in his mouth and wrapped with tape.

From the sound he realized he was in the trunk of a moving car. Hot and bound, he tried to shake himself into conscious thought. He also tried to wiggle loose from first his hands, then his legs but no use.

Every time the vehicle rounded a corner he slid across the trunk and hit the other side. He felt drowsy and wanted to sleep again, remembering the men has injected some drug into him – he was still loaded up on whatever it was.

Each time the car accelerated, Jim slammed into the back, then braced for the punishment from the inevitable braking that occurred next. In the short stretches of calm, Jim thought of the sensory deprivation tanks he'd read about. After what seemed like hours of bruising lurches, the vehicle slowed to a stop. Jim could hear the scraping of what might be gates and voices from within and without the vehicle. Then the car stopped and he waited in dread.

A rush of fresh air accompanied the sound of the trunk lid opening. The air was hot but not like the stale oven he'd been in for goodness knows how long.

"Here, roll over on your side and face me," came a coarse voice. Jim didn't move at all. A strong hand cuffed him on the side of the head and repeated the command to roll over. Jim did so immediately. "Ah, your training begins, little rabbit!" He heard followed by laughter from several voices. Humiliated, Jim rolled his face toward the voice. He felt fingers working at the ends of the tape around his head then suddenly ripping it loose, succeeding in pulling the tape halfway off.

"AAAHHHGGG." The muffled scream came from Jim.

"So sorry, rabbit. Here, let's get it all off."

He tugged it the rest of the way, removing the tape from his eyes and mouth. Jim spat the rag out and breathed the stale, hot air.

"What in the world is going on here? Where are we? Untie my hands, now!" shouted Jim, not expecting an answer or to be untied. Jim looked around and saw they had driven right into a dark stone-walled structure. A sliding garage door sealed both black Mercedes Benz inside. A fluorescent light high in the ceiling shed enough light into the room to see stone walls and a cement floor.

The big man in the suit with the banana stain grabbed Jim's arm and hustled him around the car. "This way." Another man opened a heavy metal door at the far end of the large warehouse. They shoved Jim through it.

It was cooler here. In fact, it was starting to feel really cold, Jim thought as they descended a long cinder block stairway. A short distance down the hall and they opened another heavy metal door, dragging Jim inside. A single low wattage light bulb hung from the ceiling. A wide stainless steel cabinet about seven feet tall sat closed in the corner of the room by a stainless steel sink and washboard.

In the center of the room were two bulky wooden electric chairs bolted to the floor. They were facing each other and someone was sitting in the chair with its back to the door. Leather straps and wires dangled from the unoccupied chair. Jim stiffened and tried to resist, but it was clear he was way outnumbered. He headed toward this chair and shivered as strong hands held him down and strapped him into the torture chamber. Never had he been this frightened in his life.

His eyes darted from his captors to the horrifying sight of his own hands being strapped down on the blood-spattered arms of the chair. It was then that he saw the person seated opposite him. There, facing him, strapped in as tightly as he was about to be, was Dr. Sara Einstein!

Their eyes met. Jim could see she was as scared as he was. He wanted to ask if she was okay, but knew she couldn't reply. And anyway, what kind of a question was that in these circumstances? Even if she was all right, it didn't appear as though things would remain that way for long.

When he was secured in the hard wooden chair, one of the other men - Jim supposed it was the man who sat in the back of the Mercedes when they came upon him - picked up a phone and waited. Then he reported into the phone, "Mahmoudi here. We are ready down here, sir."

The icy air penetrated Jim's light clothing and another shiver went through him, amplifying the tension and fear he felt. Jim tried to smile at Sara who nodded. Was she drugged? Does she even recognize me?" he wondered.

The men stood silent against one wall of the room. They had been chatty and noisy with plenty of rough talk until entering this torture chamber. Jim wondered if there was a recording device here. The silence was broken by the creak of the metal door.

It swung open full around on its hinges. In walked an immaculately dressed Middle Eastern man who was not smiling.

"Hello Jim," he introduced himself and extended his hand like it was a business handshake. He walked directly toward Jim. "Oh, of course, you cannot shake my hand so easily as you are enjoying my special seating arrangement," he said.

"I see you've already had a chance to say hello to Dr. Einstein," he gestured in her direction but never looked around.

"What do you want from me, and who are you?"

Kalil looked at the henchmen behind him and said in a loud voice, "Did you not inform my guest about this meeting?" No one spoke.

"You really must excuse my hospitality committee. It seems they overlooked the proper introductions. My name is Kalil. I am a collector of fine antiquities. My clients have a passion for the very unusual and pay me well for the, shall we say, unique acquisition methods necessary to procure them. That is who I am.

"You are here, and in case you aren't sure where here is, you are no longer in Israel; you are at my home in Libya. You've been unconscious for a while. They tell me that you even slept right through a nice airplane ride. Anyway, you are here to assist me in determining the location of a very important set of items you have been pursuing with some fellows from the Safari Adventure Company."

"I'm not going to be able to help you very much, Kalil. I don't know anything about where the things are, and if I did, I certainly wouldn't tell you," said Jim.

"I believe we've already anticipated your reluctance to help, and have come up with some powerful motivating reasons to persuade you. But before we begin that process, tell me why you wouldn't be willing to help me, Jim?"

"You want to hide the items in the Ancient Library, you want to make a buck off them and sell them to people who will hide them away and not let the truth or the beauty or the faith they could inspire to be shown to the world. You don't know how important these 'items' as you call them, really are."

"I am very aware of their value."

"Not monetary value, but a much, much bigger value to the world. You don't understand anything."

"Enough of this. We know that you are using that Rabbi Sol to translate the documents in your possession. I have one simple question. Where is this Ancient Library?"

"I do not know, and that's the truth."

Kalil motioned for someone behind the chair. "Mahmoudi, please. This man has volunteered to assist me today in helping your memory."

When the big man stepped around into his view Jim realized that Mahmoudi was the commando from the cave he'd whacked on the head back in the cave. He and placed both of his large hands around

Jim's throat tightly enough to hurt a lot. It was obvious he could squeeze a lot harder than he was.

"Look around you, Jim. See this place you are in. This room is deep underground. The door is sound proof. These German electric chairs are fully operational, in case you were wondering. Depending on the amount of current we choose to send to them you can experience a range of sensations from crippling pain to a slow death, frying in your own skin.

"Open that cabinet," Kalil motioned to another of his men who turned the handle on the stainless steel doors. Inside were a collection of shining chrome and stainless steel surgical instruments along with larger tools made for a butcher shop.

The tightening grip of Mahmoudi's hands around his neck forced the blood to stop flowing in Jim's head. He thought it might explode.

Can you not understand what the purpose of this room? Look at the blood on the arm of the very chair in which you are sitting. You sissy American with your civil liberties and freedom of blabbering idiots. Can you even, for a moment, conceive of the kind of people who would construct and supply such a room? This you had better do now. My soldiers and I *will* torture you, to death of necessary, in order to get what we want. And if we kill you in the process, then such is the nature of the work. We will simply find Weinberg or one of your other friends, and repeat the process.

"However, today I have an opportunity to make this interrogation a lot more interesting. Can you guess what I'm thinking? Relax your grip on our guest, please, Mahmoudi. I've decided to torture the girl here while you watch." Kalil smiled and turned away from Jim to Sara.

"Sara, Sara…you have been such a good employee up until lately."

"Employee?" said Jim.

"Yes, once she realized that I had her father working here as a translator, and that I would be somewhat reluctant to let him leave unless she cooperated, she made an excellent reporter of the entire dig on Akatori."

Jim began to put the puzzle together. So that is how the commandos found them so quickly in Sylvus's house.

"But now, since the raid, this one has been a terrible houseguest. She should make excellent sport, don't you think? So strong and arrogant. It will be a fine thing to remind her of a woman's place in the world."

"No!" Jim shouted.

"Remember, I have but one question for you, Jim. Should you be willing to answer that question, just feel free to shout out anytime. Okay? Use as much volume as you like because it really doesn't matter down here. In fact, it makes the whole process more interesting if you scream."

"Please don't hurt her…"

"Now to the Doctor." Kalil turned again to face Sara. Her eyes were wide with fear. Kalil tore the tape from her mouth in one quick jerking motion.

"You worthless devil. I hate you, do you know that?" she started.

"I think she is thirsty, so let's begin with the water."

Another of Kalil's men brought a hose around from the sink. As the others moved quickly away from her, he opened it up on Sara. The hose shot a blasting force of water onto her chest and face, but instead of screaming, she sucked in a fast breath and closed her eyes. Jets of water glanced off her body and the chair, and splashed back on Jim. The water was icy cold. Finally, the dousing stopped and Sara sat dripping in the chair completely drenched, but still defiant.

Jim could feel the places where the water hit him begin to chill in the frigid air of the room. He knew Sara must be miserably cold. Her set jaw began to shiver, then her shoulders. He had to help her somehow.

"We simply must get you out of these wet things now. Gentlemen." He motioned to two of his men who came around the chair on either side of her. They each produced knives and set them at the cuff of her khaki pant legs and then began tearing the fabric upwards, exposing her legs.

"Careful now, don't cut her yet. Take your time and do this right," Kalil said.

The men put their knives away. One of them gripped the torn fabric in each hand, squared his feet and, with a loud rip, tore the pants leg all the way up past her knee. Then he repeated the action with the other leg. Jim saw the mark of the long scarlet cut that Larson had bandaged on her leg just days ago in the cave. She sat helpless and exposed in the chair, bound by leather straps to the wooden electric chair at the ankles, waist, and wrists. She clenched her jaw tighter but could not stave off the shivering cold that made her tremble all over. The only sound was from the water splashing down to the gray concrete floor and gurgling into a drain in the center of the room.

Jim sat in shock as they produced a power saw from the cabinet. Mahmoudi plugged it into a heavy-duty extension cord and tested it with a squeeze of the trigger. The saw was exactly like the one Jim used at home to cut lumber for handyman projects around the house. It had an 8" circular blade and sharp jagged teeth, perfect for tearing through almost any construction material. The gigantic Mahmoudi gunned the blade again. The high-pitched shrieking of the blade pierced the room with a deafening screech.

"Ordinarily I would enjoy taking my time with a thing like this. It's a rare pleasure and we don't often get such delightful participants as Sara down here. But I am a busy man and the time is wasting to get this project completed. So we are just going to have to get busy fast. Bring the saw here so Jim can get a closer look."

Mahmoudi brought the saw to within an inch of Jim's face and pressed the trigger. Jim clenched his eyes shut tight but could feel the wind created by the spinning blades across his face and blowing his hair back. The force of the sound tore at his ears. Finally, he stopped and lowered the blade, returning to Sara.

"This is what we will do," Kalil spoke directly to Jim. "I will ask you to tell me the location of the Library. If you tell me, you will both be blindfolded and taken far from here and released unhurt. By the time you can re-contact your friends with the Safari Adventure Company, I will have already gotten what I seek and this will be part of the past.

"If you refuse to tell me, I will instruct Mahmoudi to saw off one of Sara's legs." Jim's heart skipped a beat at the words. "She will receive a tourniquet and be bandaged so that she will not die. If necessary, she'll be given an injection to keep her awake during the questioning.

"We will then repeat the process. I will ask again and depending on your response, we will release you or saw off the other leg." Kalil continued to describe the horribly brutal plan with dead calm. "We will continue the questions and cut off her arms. Of course by then, it may be very difficult to keep her conscious or perhaps even alive but we need not linger long between the questions and your chance to reply. This can move along a lot more rapidly than you would imagine. You are imagining this now, aren't you, Jim?"

Jim glared at Kalil. He looked at Sara who only shook her head "no" and mouthed the words. "Don't tell him." Mahmoudi sat the saw down on the table by the cabinet and pulled a rubber apron over his head. Jim fought to speak.

"What makes you think I know anything? I mean, I am just a grunt on this thing. I only happened to be along in the cave because I was in the wrong place at the wrong time. I'm not an archaeologist. Hey, I didn't even do that well in geography! If they had told me it was in some city over here, I wouldn't likely even know the name of the country. I never did memorize all the state capitals of the United States and there were only fifty of them."

"To be perfectly honest with you, Jim, I don't know if you know or not, but I am confident you will tell me what you *do* know in a very short time. As soon as we have turned Sara into a torso, we will do the same thing to you. Once the place gets messed up, it's not much more to clean up after two. This is really a great plan, you know, because if you don't have anything to tell me, then I've eliminated you as a witness anyway and reduced the size of the opposition. Larson and Weinberg will probably spend a great deal of time looking for you and that will work to my advantage, too.

"Shall we?" Kalil spoke to Mahmoudi who had donned clear plastic goggles to go with the apron. He picked up the saw and moved toward Sara. Her eyes were wild with fear, she was shivering worse than ever. The other two men shifted their weight nervously and stepped back from what was about to happen.

Jim's thoughts flashed for a moment to the video he had seen at the hotel in Cairo about the archaeological treasures. He imagined these treasures in the hands of Kalil and his so-called clients. The thought made him sick. The vision he had held from the start of the journey replayed one more time. He was descending into some mysterious candle-lit chamber.

There were the possessions of Jesus and the actual manuscripts penned in the hand of the apostles. And there on the wall was a painting of the face of Christ. He would be a part of bringing this proof of faith and hope to a world that wanted answers so badly. Even more than that, the discovery would bring him the faith he had struggled and sought so desperately.

He looked at Kalil.

He thought of the Yad Vashem – the evil in the world. He thought of the faith, hope and light the discovery of the Ancient Library would bring to that world.

And he looked at Sara.

"It's in Turkey."

116

Ain't Nobody Home

"Where did you see him last?" Weinberg asked. He and Larson had returned as soon as they had heard that Jim was missing.

"The last time I saw him, we had returned from the museum yesterday afternoon," said Rabbi Sol.

"We were just inside the gates of the city. I wanted to come back here and resume working, and Jim wanted to do some more sight seeing. When we parted company, it was late afternoon I suppose."

Larson looked at his watch. "If Kalil's men picked him up, he could be anywhere by now."

"Yes, he could even be at Kalil's compound in Libya."

"I didn't know what to do. When nightfall came, I went back down to the square and walked many of the streets. I called you as soon as I was certain he was missing. I know he was in Israel without a passport. Jim told me he'd had his documents destroyed in the fire that followed the bomb at the hotel in Cairo."

"You did just fine, Sol," Weinberg patted the big man's shoulders. "But, I don't know what we can do now except wait."

"Wait! Wait for what? To find his body? Or never find it at all?" Larson was standing up, restless, angry and ready to take some kind of action.

"Larson, we really don't know where he is. We've got to use every resource the Safari Adventure Company has, call in every favor, and find him. Kalil may well be monitoring our movements. We had better turn this over to someone else and sit tight."

"I know we should, Weinberg. I am just so mad at this idiot, I want to do something"

"Poor Jim. If he is prisoner and they torture him, he doesn't even know the location of the Ancient Library. He has nothing to tell Kalil that will lead him to the new site.

"Well…" Sol leaned forward. He placed his forehead in his left hand and rubbed his temples in a circle. "I told him about the underground city in Turkey."

"Seriously?" Larson asked. He sat back down on the couch slowly.

"Yes, we were having such a great day, and he is such a wonderful fella." Sol looked at the men. "And he wanted to know so badly. So even though we weren't certain, with such a big section of the manuscripts missing, I told him what we knew."

"This is not good," said Weinberg. "What are we to do now?"

All three men sat separately in the big circle of couches in the underground residence deep beneath the city of Jerusalem. Silently they thought through their options, each turning over every scenario they could imagine.

Larson looked at the other two and spoke. "I know exactly what to do and I am going to do it." He outlined his plan to Weinberg and Rabbi Sol. They nodded in agreement. It was risky, very risky, but they could not sit and wait for Kalil to make the next move. The time for waiting had passed.

Big Action

The air in the room was so cold, Jim thought he would be able to see his breath any minute. That is, if he were still breathing. Kalil had gleaned every fact out of Jim that he could. It was not like the movies, either. In the movies, once the torture victims began to sing, the torturer stopped hurting them.

As Kalil interrogated, he continued to inflict pain on Jim, using the terror of what might come next and the gradually descending shock of the experience to strip away any duplicity Jim might be managing to use to fool him.

It was frightfully effective. He would ask Jim a question, then ask again, and motion for the Mahmoudi to strike him, which he would do with a thick piece of rubber hose. The hose stung and shocked him. He would later remember he had screamed.

Finally, when Kalil thought he had everything Jim had to give, he took the two other henchmen and left the room. Jim shivered in the electric chair, stunned and disoriented. Seated directly across the room was Sara, soaking wet. She has to be freezing, he thought, as he looked at the shredded clothing clinging to her skin.

Vaguely aware that Mahmoudi was still in the room he thought he could hear him saying something to Sara. Behind him, Jim heard banging and noise as the man rummaged in the cabinets. He was afraid to imagine what would happen next.

The big man stepped back into view moving toward Sara. He still had on the apron and goggles. An orange extension cord trailed behind him. He held the electric saw!

"What is to be done here?" The big man spoke. "Now it seems that I am the one who gets to decide. And do you know what I've decided?"

Sara was wide-eyed. She struggled in the chair again, chafing the wrists where she had been fighting the straps.

"I've decided to do what the boss told me to do. He told me to get rid of you both. That means that you are going to die. It's my lousy job to dispose of you so you can't tell anyone what you know, and so that no one will ever find you or know what happened to you."

He winked at Sara, "I'm pretty good at that, you know. I've had a fair amount of practice. But since no one will ever know what happened to you, and since it's up to me to do it, anything I want to do is up to me." The big man turned back to Jim. "You watching this, rabbit? Are you listening?" Jim glared, snorted hard, and spit the blood that had seeped into his mouth right on to the big man's neck.

"You worthless…" Jim cringed as a stinging slap came from the big meaty hand. Mahmoudi retrieved some duct tape from the bench behind Jim and wrapped his mouth hard, giving his head a rough twist to tear off the tape after he'd wound it around Jim's head.

"There, that's the way I like to work. Nice and quiet. You just sit there and watch this. Because, I will bet, you will never see anything like this again in your life as long as you live. In fact, I guarantee it!" he laughed at himself.

He turned back to Sara, "Now as I was saying, no one will ever know what we do. So you are going to be my girl friend for the night. We will have some fun and then sadly the fun will have to end, and you will have to go. You will want to leave, just like you do now, with the rabbit here." The man jerked his thumb back at Jim. "This makes me very jealous. So what can I do to remind you how much I care about you? I think I know." He reached over and picked up the electric saw and gripped it loosely in one hand, waving the heavy gray metal tool at Sara like a toy.

"I've been looking forward to this since the rabbit began to talk." The man pulled the saw down out of the air and cradled it in both hands. Slipping his right hand index finger over the trigger, he held the weight of the saw in his left palm. He pressed the trigger and the saw came to life with a sickening screech. Using the index finger of his left hand, he carefully pulled the protective guard back on the saw, exposing the jagged teeth of the whirling blades. He carefully moved the blade toward Sara's exposed legs, taunting her.

Sara screamed and tried to pull away.

Jim's muffled shout hurt his aching head.

The metal door to the chamber squeaked opened slowly.

Then, into the room stepped professor Avi. His balding spectacled head was practically dwarfed by the huge metal door, eyes wide in shock at the big man leaning toward his daughter with the power saw. How long had he focused on the archeological work Kalil put in front of him and ignored the signs all around him that he and Sara, his only daughter, were caught in the criminal's trap?

Avi moved quickly into the room and shouted, running toward the evil giant. The big man let go of the trigger and stepped back. As the sound of the saw whined down, he shouted back at Avi.

"Who are you? What are you doing here?"

"Kalil sent me down here to help you get rid of these two," Avi pretended.

"I don't get it. This isn't what we do."

"He said you'd say that." Avi looked around the room at Jim and tried to remain nonchalant in the midst of the terror he felt. He'd heard about this room but had never seen it. He had grown suspicious of his mysterious boss when Sara returned from the dig site in an emotional meltdown and refused to talk about it. Then when she disappeared from the compound yesterday, he had determined to find out for himself what was going on. When he looked out the window of his research lab and saw Kalil leave so quickly with his those two nasty ones in the helicopter, he followed the hallway he'd suspected held more than he allowed himself to know.

Now he was face to face with an enormous armed killer who was about to destroy the person he loved the most, his baby girl, and some stranger, too.

"What did Kalil tell you, professor, and why are you in on this? This isn't your side of the street, if you know what I mean." The big man took the situation seriously. All the power he had felt alone in the room with his two victims was nothing compared to the fear he had of what Kalil might do if he chose to punish him. The professor was part of the elite group in the office, not a dirty work grunt like him.

"He said you would probably make a big mess and take forever and that he didn't want that to happen." Professor Avi moved around the room behind Jim's chair as he spoke. The thin man was observing the room and taking a scientific inventory. Unlike the lab, though, he had only a few seconds to think of what to do. He lowered his voice to its toughest growl. "He wanted these two to be gone quickly. So let's get this over with."

"And do what?" Mahmoudi asked, putting the professor in charge.

"Let's kill them here," he said in his toughest gangster voice, "clean up the mess, and get rid of them in the usual way," though he had no idea what the usual way was, or if there was one.

Mahmoudi shrugged, disappointed. Clearly the fantasy he had dreamed up was shattered. Now it was back to work. "Okay then, I'm gonna cut her up, then him," he nodded toward Jim, "so they fit in the plastic bags in that cabinet. You don't have an apron, so stand clear."

The professor couldn't believe anyone could talk about the vicious murder of two human beings with such casual language. He might as well be doing home repair. He steeled himself for what he knew he must do next. Avi picked up the hose. "I'll rinse things down so we aren't tramping around in a big mess."

"Okay, but be careful with that thing. I'm plugged in you know?" Mahmoudi nodded toward the orange extension cord.

"Got ya."

Mahmoudi powered up the saw again.

Faster than he'd moved since he was a boy, the professor leaped into a shooter's stance with his weight spread solidly on the balls of his feet. He took the nozzle of the hose in both hands and squeezed as hard as he could. The solid stream of water hit its target with perfection – right into the motor of the saw.

Instantly, 220 volts of electricity shot a lightning bolt into Mahmoudi's immense frame contracting every muscle, squeezing his finger like a vise on the trigger of the saw. Frozen in a death grip on the thing that would kill him, he lurched violently while sparks exploded from the saw, turning his arm a bluish-black. The professor pulled the stream of water away to avoid electrocuting himself. By the time the force of the shock threw the big man to the ground, his heart had already stopped beating. The saw kept going.

He landed face down with the saw underneath him. It clawed at his flesh and dug a bloody trench deep into his chest. The body twitched and convulsed on the floor.

Finally professor Avi looked up at Sara and Jim. Their attention had been riveted to the corpse. Now they both looked at the professor. Tears streamed down Sara's cheeks as her father tenderly unbuckled the straps that had held her down for hours.

"Oh my dear, dear Sara. Honey, what is happening here? What have I gotten you into, my child?"

Jim thought he'd never heard so much pain in a man's voice in his life. "You mean that all the time I have been working here, you have been going back and forth to the dig on Santorini because he told you he would kill me if you didn't?

"Yes, yes, but please, it's okay now," said Sara.

"Did the Safari Adventure Company people know this?"

"No, I've had to be like a spy for Kalil. I was hoping for a chance to figure this all out - but I never thought it would come to this."

"Oh, Sara, I'm so sorry I didn't realize…"

"It's okay Papa. It's fine now."

He finished unbuckling her from the chair and then released Jim. By the time Jim was free, she had told her father about the raid and the burglary at the cave. He nodded when they told him about the Ancient Library.

"We pieced together the manuscripts as best as we could and determined that the Ancient Library is buried on a lower level in the old Underground City of Kaymakli in Turkey. Without the scrolls that Kalil stole, we could not be certain."

"Yeah," said Jim staring down the body of the man who would have killed him, "and I have sent Kalil right to the exact location."

"But you saved my life." Sara kissed his bruised cheek.

"And so did you, Papa." She hugged her father with both arms around his neck.

"There is no one in the compound right now except us," Professor Avi said, wiping his hands on his pants. "I suggest we get out of here now before Kalil or someone returns and finds us."

Without looking back, they rounded the metal door and took the stairs back to the main house. Jim marveled at the elaborate palace. It was hard to believe a torture chamber was but a few feet away from this serene and beautiful palace. How ironic that abundant life and dark death could be so close together like this, invisible to one another.

"I must get my things," Professor Avi said, almost running up the stairs to the second floor toward his office.

"No, Papa," yelled Sara, "we need to get out of here now!"

"I know! I know!" the professor's voice echoed down the hall. "Just got to grab a couple of things."

"Do you know your way around this place?" asked Jim.

"Yes, I do."

"Then tell me where the heck the bathroom is!" he said. "This isn't like the movies. I've really had to go for a long time."

"Really, me too." She pointed him in the right direction and ran off. In a few minutes they joined back at the entrance, but Sara's father was not there. He reappeared in a few moments clutching a battered brown leather duffel bag. "Well, if you are waiting on me, you are backing up!" he practically shouted as headed to the door.

"Let's go." Sara opened the door and they stepped into a brilliant Egyptian dawn.

"I...SAID...THIS...IS...CRAZY!" the helicopter pilot screamed into his headset microphone loud enough for Larson to hear over the roar of the engines. Tyler had been a helicopter pilot in Vietnam and had seen a lot of risky landings. At this point, he tried to be a lot more careful. Larson just shrugged the determined gesture of a person who has chosen to take on a grim task, and moved well past the question of whether or not to turn back.

He pulled the tiny microphone on his headset closer to his mouth and shouted back. "THEY WILL NEVER EXPECT US TO COME IN LIKE THIS."

"HE'S RIGHT!" shouted Weinberg, the determination and excitement showing in his face. Larson looked back at the team. Except for Weinberg, Tyler, Larson, and the two others were ex-Navy Seals. They were highly trained and equipped for action. But Tyler was right, this was risky because they were going in without knowing what size of force they faced or, worse yet, how well equipped they were.

Based on the briefing Larson got about the raid on Toussaint's dig site, if Kalil's troops were home, they could have some nasty firepower. One thing he'd learned in his covert ops training, and in business ventures afterward: Never under-estimate the power of complete surprise. History was replete with stories of a tiny force whipping overwhelming odds. General George Washington would have gotten creamed if he'd fought the British at noon on a non-holiday. Crossing the Delaware River on Christmas Eve tipped the odds in his favor and a nation was born.

"At this altitude," Larson spoke into his microphone again, "no radar will catch us. They will have to have a visual. We will be coming in with the sun to our backs. That is all we'll need to get on the ground and do our thing." The men in the back of the chopper checked their weapons one more time.

"Okay, it's just ahead. Here we go." Tyler banked the helicopter around and dropped it just above the palm trees at the perimeter of the compound. There was no gunfire, and no one even in sight. A helicopter pad was clearly visible, minus its helicopter.

"Set us down there." Larson pointed toward the fountains amid a wide, manicured lawn.

"Wait, what's that?" the pilot shouted.

The front door of the gigantic house opened and out walked, or limped, a woman and two men. They stopped in their tracks and shielded their eyes from the bright rising sun. The older man ran back into the house but the other man and the woman began waving.

"It's Kalil!" Professor Avi shouted, running back into the house for cover.

"Wait a minute," Sara yelled back, straining to see the helicopter through the brilliant glare of the sun. "Its maroon. Jim! Papa! It's a Safari Adventure Company helicopter!"

"I'll go get him. You let them know it's us!" Jim shouted.

Sara began waving, peering hard through the bubble in the front of the helicopter to see if he was in there. "Larson, you are truly amazing." She said as she shook her head.

"All alert!" Larson's hoarse yell came through their headsets. Weinberg and the others, bulletproof vests, helmets and sunglasses in place, rose to one knee and sighted through their weapons. "This could be a trap! Keep the chopper on full ready, Tyler!"

"I can't believe what I am seeing," Larson whispered. "Its her!" he roared and leaped from the deck of the chopper. The other two men in the back jumped out on the ground and fanned their weapons side to side, eyes searching for trouble and prepared to return fire in any direction.

"This will be a story to tell now, won't it?" Weinberg said with a smile into the microphone. The pilot gripped the joystick and searched the sky nervously, hoping they were alone.

Before he got to her, he could see she'd been roughed up. Larson, the big athletic ex-football jock, scooped Dr. Sara Einstein up in his arms and hustled her to the helicopter.

"You clothes are wet," he said.

"You wouldn't believe what we've been through." She clung to his neck as he ran. When he sat her down in the back of the helicopter, she realized how utterly exhausted she was.

When everyone was aboard, the two armed men jumped up on the flight deck. Weinberg gave a quick thumbs-up to Tyler. The engines screamed into high gear and the chopper was airborne in a flash. The shooters scanned the site for trouble, but none came. When everyone was buckled in and the aircraft was climbing to a higher altitude, relief and the hugeness of what had just happened hit the rescuers and the rescued.

"How in the world did you just happen to land as we came walking out of the house?" asked Sara.

"How in the world didn't you show up a couple of hours earlier!" said Jim, half joking.

"Larson just figured that the only place we knew to look was Kalil's compound. It was a complete roll of the dice to try to come here," Weinberg said. "We had no idea what we'd find, if anything at all."

"If you'd have been here earlier, you'd have been shot out of the sky," said Professor Avi, clutching his briefcase in his lap. "Kalil's entire little army was here until they rushed off just a bit ago."

Sara introduced her father to Larson and Weinberg. As the helicopter reached its cruising altitude, everyone settled down and tried to relax. Weinberg passed water around to Jim, Sara and Avi.

Sara leaned into Larson and began to talk to him loudly enough that he could hear but softly enough that the others could not. Jim knew she must be telling him how she had been blackmailed into working for Kalil. It must have been terrible to keep a secret like that while working on the dig, and fearing that your father would be killed.

"That explains everything now," said Larson. Looking deep into the eyes his instincts had been unable to trust completely.

"I'm so sorry," she said. "More than anything, I wanted to be a part of this important work. If you'll let me, I still do."

"It doesn't look like that is going to happen now. We are going to have to figure out a completely new plan. Turkey is a terrible place for Westerners but Kalil has a gigantic network there. He's probably already got the area around the site shut down for himself and equipment on the way.

"We have all done the best we could. If it is fate and God's will that Kalil gets to the Ancient Library, and even if he plunders the whole thing, we must keep it in perspective. God is in control of all things and He will use this for His glory in a way we may never understand." Weinberg's calming voice came across their headsets tinny - like AM gospel radio.

"Don't be so certain," Sara's father spoke up. He patted the leather bag he'd been clutching since leaving the palace.

"I say, Professor Avi, what have you got in that interesting-looking bag there?" Weinberg asked.

"Yes, Papa, what in the world did you run back to your office to get?"

"Just a few letters from an old friend," Avi said.

"What kinds of letters are so important that you'd risk your life to save them?" Jim asked.

Professor Avi reached into the faded leather duffel bag and produced a high-tech stainless steel cylinder. "An old business man from the first century named Sylvus."

"What?" Sara sat up straight.

"That's right," Avi held the cylinder up victoriously, "I have stolen the missing manuscripts from that Son of Satan, Kalil. I translated them last night and I know the precise location of the Ancient Library.

"Oh my God!" shouted Jim, "Is Kalil on the way there now?"

"No. I sent him off on a wild goose chase." The professor pulled himself up and spoke as if he were giving a lecture at the university. "He came to me and asked about the likelihood of the Turkish location. I confirmed it. Let Kalil dig up the entire Underground City in Turkey. The greatest archaeological discovery in the history of mankind is near the confluence of the Tigris and Euphrates in Ancient Babylon."

Everyone but Jim said, "A-ha!

"What does that mean?" Jim turned to Weinberg. "Where is he talking about?"

"Jimmy, my boy, Ancient Babylon is modern Iraq."

By The Rivers of Babylon

To my dear entrusted servant and co-laborer Justinius. Greetings to you from my own hand, Sylvus of Akatori.

It seemed prudent to leave the misleading scroll behind to forestall any pursuit by the Roman soldiers. Now that we are aboard the ship and underway, I've composed this letter to tell you where the actual collection will be taken.

I've secured a place in a caravan with a trusted old friend who has made many business trips for me to the lands East. We will travel with the collection across the Northern route through Assyria and into Northern Babylonia. There we will leave the caravan, which is bound for Babylon itself, and continue on to a monastery deep in the mountains.

A certain number of monks have begun a cell there led by a believer exiled from Jerusalem named Bartholomew. They have discovered a network of caves in what was once an old military outpost. The Roman army has lost interest in this area. The people and the land are too fierce and rugged. The upper caves are dry and arid. I believe the treasures we carry will be safe from weather and time there. It is so far out of the way of things the Library of God can rest peacefully until a safer time.

When we arrive in Seleucia I will send this letter back with the captain, to be returned through the tunnel to the original hiding place. If you are reading this, you will have already found it. My love to you and to your family, until we meet again in this life or heaven beyond. Blessings and peace be to you always.

By Horseback

The craggy foothills leading into the mountainous area of Northern Iraq were made up of impossibly odd-shaped gray stones protruding through the lush green grass. This land was good for goat grazing, that was for certain. The small farms they had passed were neatly tucked into the wider areas where the soil outnumbered the rocks. It had to be tilled by hand or oxen.

Jim unfolded the report he'd removed from his green canvas backpack. If ever he had wanted to insert himself into both the reality of the world and the reality of the history of the Bible, it was right here, right now. He looked across the campsite. It was hard to believe he was really here.

He began to read about their destination.

Baghdad, Iraq sits on the land once occupied by the fabled city of Babylon, the capital of the ancient Kingdom of Babylonia. The fertile delta between the Tigris and Euphrates rivers where most biblical scholars agree the real Garden of Eden once was is the home of many of the first chapters of early human history.

Herein lies the city of Ninevah where Jonah reluctantly went to preach after being convinced how serious God was while in the belly of the great fish. The tower of Babel is in the region. Abraham was born and lived much of his life in Ur of The Caldees (Genesis 11:28), which was located near the Euphrates River approximately two hundred miles to the Southeast.

Nineveh, located on the Tigris River, was the capital of the brutal expansionist Assyrian empire. The Assyrian army traveled all the way to the northern kingdom of Israel, conquered and transported the "Lost Ten Tribes" into exile, never to return (2 Kings 17:21-23).

The Babylonians conquered the Southern kingdom of Judah, destroyed the original Temple at Jerusalem, and carried the people of Judah away into exile (2nd Chronicles 36:15-20.) They remained there until the Babylonian empire fell to the Persians who allowed the Jewish people to return to Israel (2nd Chronicles 36:20-23)

Two hundred fifty miles north of Baghdad sits the third largest city in Iraq, Masul. The city was an important trade center in the Abbasid era because of its strategic position on the caravan route between India, Persia, and the Mediterranean.

Masul's chief export was cotton. Today's word muslin is derived from the name of this very city. In the 13th century, Masul was almost completely destroyed by the Mongol invasion, but rebuilding and revival began under Ottoman rule. Masul was once a walled city, and the remains of part of the city wall are still in existence at Bash Tapia castle, on the western bank of the Tigris.

An ethnically diverse city, Masul has the highest proportion of Christians of all the Iraqi cities. It contains several interesting old churches, including the Clock and Latin Church, which has some fine marble and stained glass. The Chaldean Catholic Church of Al-Tahira was built as a monastery in AD 300 and became a church in 1600 when various additions were built.

An interesting mosque in the city is the Mosque of Nebi Yunus, said to be the burial place of the Biblical Jonah. It is built on a mound beneath which are thought to be part of the ruins of the ancient city of Nineveh. Any attempt to verify this is impossible, however, as the site is sacred and cannot be disturbed.

Thirty four miles north of Masul is the centuries-old monastery of Dair Rabban Hurmiz, the most famous and frequently visited monastery in Iraq. Dair Rabban Hurmiz was the holy seat of the Patriarch of the Assyrian Church of the East for several generations. Situated directly above a large cave in the Alqush mountain, the monastery overlooks a famous valley called Gali Al-dair meaning "valley of the monastery." The Chaldean Church, previously the Church of the East, cares for it.

The monastery is unreachable by automobile and has no electricity or running water. The monks rely on mountain springs and oil lamps for everyday life. Plans to build a road to the sacred site have been delayed for more than ten years, the funds being diverted instead to the wildly aggressive military passion of the Iraqi leader.

The professors, Avi and Sol, had worked non-stop to give the team a reliable map. The scholars had begged to make the journey but Larson had insisted they remain behind. The fewer people sneaking into Iraq the better. He had promised them that they would be the first to analyze the materials should they be fortunate enough to find the Library.

Weinberg and Toussaint were preparing a meal over a small gas-powered stove. Toussaint had insisted on coming along despite taking a beating at Kalil's hands in the island attack on the site. He had only just had the stitches out of his ear and sported a bandage across it. His injury was a source of both teasing and sympathy. Everyone in the team had suffered at the hands of Kalil; Toussaint's ear was a visible reminder of that.

Jim watched the two men working together. They were having a good time. No doubt they were buoyed along through the inconveniences of this kind of travel by the prospect of what might lit at the end of their journey. Jim stood up, stretched his long legs, and joined Sara and Larson who were feeding the horses and getting them ready for the day's ride.

"If things go well, we will reach the monastery before dark," Weinberg said as he dished up some hot oatmeal from the pan on the stove. He dropped in some sugar and powdered milk, then sat back down on his sleeping bag.

"You mean if we do not get lost again today," Toussaint teased Larson.

"No kidding." Larson replied. "This is not the easiest place to navigate and the maps are the worst ones I have ever seen. We did a lot of bad terrain navigation when I was a Navy Seal but we had the best maps the U.S. Government could produce."

"Still, it would help if you could read your compass, Larson." Toussaint wouldn't let him off the hook for his error.

"Okay, okay. I thought you guys roughed me up enough about it yesterday."

"You are doing a fine job, Larson. Don't let the amateurs give you a hard time," said Weinberg.

"I still can't believe we are here," said Sara. "To think that a few days ago we were in Kalil's compound on the edge of death just blows me away."

"It's going to be a long time before I can lie down to sleep and not have that scene in the dungeon in my mind," said Jim. Sara nodded. "A very long time."

"But, indeed, we are here, and Kalil is not. And everyone has had a part in making this all possible. I have the greatest sense that what we are about to do and discover, is going to have a serious impact on archaeology, the fabric of history and the world.

"Yes, I can almost touch the artifacts," said Toussaint.

They cleared the campsite, loaded their gear on the horses and, one by one, dropped down the path out of the clearing and into the blue shadows of the morning. Garbed in the robes and headgear of the locals, Sara carefully dressed as a pious local woman. She even had a scarf for covering her face. She kept it handy so she could slip it up in place at a moments notice. The group appeared to be a small family of travelers moving slowly through the rugged land.

Hidden deep in Weinberg's saddlebag was the map that Sol and Avi had drawn from the description in Sylvus's scroll. Sara led the translation. Every time they drifted off into hypothesis, she brought them gently back to the task at hand. Though they had never met before, their mutual love of the work had made them fast friends. It was a joy to see them digging into the scrolls together, even though Jim could hardly understand much of what they were talking about!

Weinberg and Jim were traveling together again, this time through the arid steppes of Northern Iraq by horseback. It is illegal for foreigners to travel here without express permission of the Iraqi government. The Safari Adventure Company was really well connected to get into a country that was on the verge of another war. But as much as he was excited by the idea of it all, the physical part of the journey was starting to get to Jim.

How did they stand it? He thought of cowboys in the movies he'd watched as a boy. They just rode along, seemingly forever, on horseback and only fell out of the saddle after an all-nighter with an arrow or two sticking out of them.

"How did they stand it?" asked Jim wearily.

"Who?"

"The cowboys?"

"What do you mean? "

"This constant, life-destroying butt-stress," said Jim as he shifted his weight in the saddle for the millionth time."

Toussaint laughed, snorted actually. Jim always thought Toussaint was just on the verge of saying "le-haw-haw-haw" any minute in the most characteristic Pepe Le Pew French accent. "Life destroying butt-stress!" he repeated and snorted again. "Messier Jim, you have the most, how would one say, unique vocabulary I've ever heard."

Haven't you seen any of the old spaghetti Westerns, Toussaint?"

"Spaghetti what?"

"Western's. American's made a lot of films in Italy about the cowboy days. It saved them a lot of money."

"Where are you going with this, Jim?" asked Weinberg. You know, in those movies, the cowboys, bad guys and good, would ride for like weeks at a time, and the only time they would get off these grinder horses would be when they rode up to a saloon with a couple of arrows sticking out of them."

"Still, you would agree, it is better than walking all this way. No?" Toussaint said.

"Yeah, I guess so. But if I were walking, I would be strengthening my legs and when it was over I could walk even better. There is a very real possibility that when I get off Widow Maker here," Jim patted his horse tossed the mane playfully, "no offense buddy, I may never be able to walk normally again.

"You my friend, have entirely too much time to think about what is wrong," said Toussaint.

"What else am I to think about?"

"Why don't you try counting your blessings?" suggested Weinberg.

"Are you kidding?" said Jim.

"I am serious."

"We are somewhere in the middle of this God-forsaken desert, straddling bony horses, our food and water are running out, and if we are really lucky we will encounter a guy who has us out-gunned, out-supplied and wants to kill us. Yeah, we are truly blessed."

"You are one of the luckiest people alive and you don't even know it," Weinberg said.

"He's right, you know," Toussaint added.

"Oh here we go, Jim said with a sigh, resigned to another of Weinberg's philosophical dissertations.

"If you don't want to hear this, you don't have to," Weinberg said.

"Well, let me check my day planner for this time frame," Jim pretended to thumb through an invisible book. "Nope, looks like we have an opening here for you, Weinberg. Please proceed."

Weinberg thought for a moment, then spoke. "If you found out you were a millionaire today..."

"*Then* I'd have some blessings to count," Jim interrupted.

He looked at Toussaint for a laugh but Toussaint only shook his head.

"But my friend, you are already a millionaire and you don't even know it yet." Weinberg continued.

"Oh yeah, how so?"

"You have two eyes, don't you?"

"Sure," Jim played along.

"Well, what would you take for one of them?"

"Seriously?"

"Seriously. $50,000... $100,000, or more. How much would you take for the pair? Then let's move on to fingers and the larger limbs."

"Well if you think about it like that..."

"The whole point *is* for you to think about it like that! Like many of your countrymen, you just take so much for granted. Am I right, Toussaint?"

"I wept because I had no DVD...," Toussaint sighed with a serious face, "until I met a man who had no VCR."

Jim snorted at the play on an old platitude.

"That sums up the consumerism of the Western mind pretty well doesn't it?" Weinberg said. "We overeat, over-entertain, over-consume, over-stimulate and still we want more. You own, and have experienced so much more than any generation in history, and still you only see that which you lack."

Weinberg was on a roll now. He had Jim's attention. In a way, it seemed like a healing moment. Jim had missed the wisdom of the friendly Englishman. Jim smiled. He felt as though he had a second chance to pick up where they had left off in Africa before tragedy had struck.

No matter how this adventure ended, he knew he had been given a once-in-a-lifetime opportunity. Here he was, experiencing again the feeling that has lifted his heart and set him on the journey of knowing himself.

This only served to make him grateful for the moment, for the time, for the chance. He smiled again, because he understood in a deeper way what Weinberg was saying, even though it came in a different context than even his teacher would know. Good teachers are like that, though. They spin their words in a way that provokes your own mind to fashion the lesson that connects.

"So you see, my dear Jim," Weinberg's use of Jim's name brought him back to the moment. "You are busy whining about your horse while all around you are good things you've chosen to ignore."

"You are right," said Jim.

"What?"

"Please continue."

"Yes, well, that is…what I mean to say is that the mind can only contain one thing at a time: positive or negative, not both. You cannot stop thinking negatively by just saying you will. You must replace the negative with a new and positive thought. Then the dominant emotion can accompany that thought. The Bible says…"

Not the Bible again, Jim turned his head and rolled his eyes. Does this guy have anything that doesn't summon a verse?

"…whatever is good, whatever is lovely, of good report, whatever is pure…think on these things," Weinberg clapped his hands for emphasis. "There is not much better advice for a positive attitude than these words."

"Okay, seriously," Jim interrupted. "Are you actually riding along just now ignoring the discomfort of these horses and the grimness of our situation because you are thinking of little verses?"

"Actually," Weinberg turned and faced Jim with a serious but caring look, "I feel every bump, every hardship that you feel, Jim. Perhaps even more since I am a few years your senior… *junior*!"

Jim looked down.

"But I am actually thinking right now about solutions, expectations, possibilities of success and what we'll find in the Library. And the serene beauty of this place I've never been in my life. Quite honestly, the little verses that pop into my head because I took the time to memorize them comfort me with the truth. I am lifted up, even out of this saddle, by the majesty of God's word for me at that moment. And the fact that no matter what happens on the other side of that mountain, I know how this entire thing, this world, ends up."

"Okay I will buy all the rest, but calling this place beautiful?"

"Look past your nose, my friend," Weinberg swept his hand in a wide arc. "The dark mountains in the distance, the pale wisp of a moon not yet set from the sky nor quite made invisible by the sunlight.

It is all quite beautiful. Have you noticed the color of the soil here? Or that there are a thousand kinds of plants that live here, that eke out their existence in grace and beauty despite the impossibility of what we think of as growing conditions?

"You've probably missed most of the two dozen or so lizards and three snakes I've counted scurrying across our path in the last two hours..."

"You've seen snakes?" Jim asked, scanning the ground all around them frantically.

"And spiny lizards," added Toussaint.

"What kind of lizards?" asked Jim, still checking the ground and worrying.

"The point is that the courage, strength, energy, and attitude we develop is shaped by the attitude we nurture or destroy by our focus. In this way, we choose our potential success or ordain our failure."

"He's right you know," Toussaint added. "If an archaeologist required instant gratification, most of what we discover would lie buried forever. If we focused upon the dust, the hard work, and high percentage of failure, we would all give up and what good would that do? I believe this is one reason it is imperative to have a sense of romance about our work; that we love what we do. That love of the doing is usually a blend of the joy of the day-to-day, but mostly seeing the end result we are creating.

"As I add to the knowledge of the world, I add to the wisdom of my own life. The questions we answer only bring more questions, different questions," Toussaint concluded.

"And if I may say, Jimmy boy," Weinberg spoke again, "there are quite a lot of people in this world who would trade places with you gladly for the chance at a chance possibility of glimpsing the treasures of the library. Wouldn't you agree?"

"Yes," Jim added. "One of them was me a few days ago back at the helicopter hanger in Jerusalem.

They rode on in silence.

"Oh yes," said Weinberg, "one thing more."

Both Jim and Toussaint laughed together.

"This is not a God-forsaken place. The only place that God forsakes..."

"Wait a minute, Weinberg," Jim said. "If what we find up ahead is what we are looking for, then the fundamental answer to my question about the reliability of your God, your Bible and the whole shootin' match will be over. I will believe then. But up until then, since we are so close to finding out.... could you just please not do the Bible thing on me? It's just wearing me out."

Weinberg nodded with a smile.

"Thanks," said Jim.

"Well, can I give you some advice that you really need to hear. And it's not in the Bible." asked Toussaint.

"Okay. I guess so," said Jim.

"Perhaps you should try taking your big fat American consumer wallet out of your back pocket. That will probably make your horse seem a bit less bumpy, no?"

Weinberg and Toussaint fought back laughter as long as they could, then it burst out across the desert in rolling waves. Jim fetched his wallet out of his back pocket and slipped it into the bag on the saddle, red faced and embarrassed. "Why am I even carrying my wallet out here?" he thought. "There are no ATM's for a very long way. Old habits, old ways of thinking, are very hard to kill, he thought...very hard indeed."

They rode for an hour at a time and rested as long as they needed until the sun began to fade behind them into the western sky. "If we ride all night, we can be there at dawn."

"What kind of a plan is that?" asked Jim. "If we ride all night, even the horses will be too exhausted to think."

"I was just joking, Jim. Let's camp up on the other side of that ridge there and get some rest. We can leave in the morning and get there after lunchtime tomorrow. Okay, wrangler Jim?"

"Sure, that sounds pretty good." Jim began to think about another meal of the MRE rations that Weinberg had commandeered. Gross as they were at first, Jim was starting to salivate just thinking about food. He was famished. He tried to practice being grateful for a desperate enough appetite to actually anticipate the food-like contents of the old army rations.

As they picked their way up the side of the ridge the trail widened into a sort of road. They rode on up, pressing to the top where Weinberg said they could camp.

"Look here, lads," Weinberg pulled his horse up to a stop and turned back to face the direction they had come. The sun was just about to dip behind the floor of the desert behind them. The distance they had covered a little at a time took them in. Each one, alone with their private thoughts, watched the unique moment of sunset.

The shimmering heat off the desert floor colliding with the cool air falling painted a never-ending range of color and hue in the vista. Dark blue, indigo, and violet merged with the crimson, gold, and purple of the changing world. The speed of the disappearance of the sun met the growing darkness. That miracle of nature, the human eye, did its amazing job without a conscious command from the travelers. It began to expand the tightened iris that protected it from looking directly into the fading sun, and widened it to accept the limited light from the lingering moon.

A puff of chilly wind came up out of nowhere, refreshing their faces and stirring the horses. It felt like the world had just sighed its relief of another day of toil.

"Let's go have another glorious MRE supper," said Jim, remembering his appetite.

Larson turned his horse around and took the lead up the path. "We are out of food. We ate the last of it at lunch today," he said.

"No way!" said Jim attempting to get his ride oriented to follow. "We can't be out of food?"

"We'll need to find a restaurant."

"You've got to be kidding," said Jim. "We haven't even seen a village…

His words were cut short by the sharp report of a single high-powered rifle shot. The echo clattered off the hills around them as the horse danced. They looked around frantically for the source of the shot.

"Everyone, get your horses back behind these rocks," Larson barked. He kicked his horse to action to a tall line of boulders on the left side of the trail.

No sooner had he given the order, but three men stepped from behind the very rocks he was heading for. The men were dressed in the local clothing of the Northern Kurdish tribes including the wrapped wool headpieces with the draping scarf. Two more men stepped out and joined the first three. Their faces were weathered and hardened into fierce frowns. All of the men were dressed the same and carried automatic weapons.

The last man come appear spoke to Larson and the others in a language Jim could not understand. "Sara, can you help here?" She pulled her horse up along Larson's and attempted to communicate. After three different language tries, the leader and Sara seemed to connect. They went back and forth until Sara reported to the group.

"They are Kurdish freedom fighters. They want to know what our business is here."

"Tell them we are headed to the Monastary at Masul. There's no use in lying to them; its not like we can disappear," said Larson. Sara turned back to the spokesman of the group and another barrage of language ensued. He turned back to the others in his group and spoke to them. They all seemed to agree with nodding heads and the leader turned back to Sara and spoke in English.

"My name is Samangi. Our captain has asked me to communicate with you in English. Do you understand me?" He pointed to his chest.

Everyone nodded and said yes at the same time.

"We have been keeping our eyes open for your group. The monks at Mosul are our friends. They know you are coming and we have been asked to make sure you arrive safely. Is there a scientist from France in your group?"

"Yes, that is me," Toussaint spoke and raised his hand. Everyone on both sides relaxed.

"Good. How are we to assist you?"

Larson pulled out a map and said, "For one thing, you could tell us where we are on this map and if we are going the right way."

"And how about something to eat?" asked Jim.

"Are you hungry?"

"Well, yes, actually, we could use something to eat."

"Let us prepare a meal here," Samangi said. "And we will get your map right, and give you something to fill your stomach as well. Good?"

Just a few minutes later, three four-wheel-drive trucks pulled up from the road ahead. As the dust subsided, the men pulled boxes and supplies down faster than seemed possible. In no time a camp was up, a fire was lit, and water was boiling.

During the meal, the rebels asked them many questions about the Safari Adventure Company's home countries. They were very curious about what the foreigners knew from news reports about Iraq. "We get no news except that which comes by radio sometimes. We aren't sure what to trust here from outside sources," said Samangi.

Jim tried to ask questions about the fighter's lives, but they seemed reluctant to talk. "We fight for our land – and to avenge the murder of our family and friends. Until Iraq is free of this butcher of a dictator, no one is safe here."

After the meal and a careful review of the directions to the monastery, they said their goodbyes.

"You are not too far now, and though it is growing dark, the moon will be very bright tonight. You will have no trouble making your way. Good luck and give our greetings to the brothers at Mosul." They shook hands and parted.

They followed single-file around a series of switchbacks that led farther up the mountain. The way was narrow, but just at the rebels had assured them, the bright moonlight was sufficient to see the way. Alone in his thoughts, Jim reflected on the conversation with Weinberg earlier in the day about counting his blessings and being thankful for what he had instead of what he lacked.

He had actually started to get mad at Larson back there about being hungry. Yet it wasn't his dilemma alone. Many people had been hungry before in this world, some all the time and much hungrier than he. And some people starved to death. He wasn't really in danger of that, he knew. There were many things to feel grateful for. For one thing he was here and not sitting in an office bored or stressed out of his mind.

This was his choice; he took every step of the journey by choosing to take it. Now he was doing exactly what he'd sought. He was on the verge of maybe the most important archaeological discovery of his generation, maybe of all time. He would forever be linked with the find of the century and in the midst of it all, he was getting paid...with benefits! It was the first time since fleeing Egypt that he stopped to consider he was no longer unemployed when he returned to his home. The Safari Adventure Company employed him, and the one thing he had really wanted...adventure...was right here!

Last in line, no one could see the tall American smiling in the pale light of the moon. Jim drew his horse closer to the nearest rider.

"Hey, Weinberg."

"Yes, Jim," Weinberg turned half way around to see him.

"I am so blessed to be here."

"Why, yes, you are. We all are!"

"Really, I was thinking of what you said this morning about counting our blessings and it worked. I truly feel lucky to be right at this place in exactly these beautiful circumstances right in this moment, Weinberg."

"Ahh, you don't know the half of it Jimmy, my boy," Weinberg winked and gave his little thumbs up gesture.

Jim settled back in his saddle, as happy as the slow pupil who knew the answer for a change.

The path continued around the craggy ledge. On the left, a sheer wall of rock jutted straight up to a height beyond his vision. On the right, the path melted fast to an incline too steep to walk, down to a distant valley. From this vantage point, the soft light of the full moon lit the entire scene. Jim could see for miles across the rivers and mountains of ancient Babylonia. This land was inhabited as far back as human history had been recorded. What sort of people had traveled this thin ribbon of ground around this mountain? He felt a bond with the people of the past, a brotherhood of mankind. Here in this place so different and so desolate compared with his urban American world, he felt more connected to his kind, to his humanity, than ever before.

He turned back to the path ahead. The horse had been doing all the work for some time as it carefully picked its way along following the horse in front of it. The moon slipped behind a cloud and the path ahead became much darker. Then, as if peeking its head around a corner to see them, the lights of the monastery began to appear one by one. Hundreds of little yellow flames from candles and oil lamps set in the high stone windows shone out in the darkness.

To Jim, they seemed to shine out just for him.

The Monastery at Masul

"Looks like it's open for business!" Weinberg said loud enough for the others to hear.

It did seem odd, Jim thought, that such a place should be lit up like this in the middle of the night. The path widened to an open meadow that led up to the bottom of the monastery's first level of walls and terraces. The riders drew abreast of each other.

"Yes, they were kind enough to leave the lights on for us," said Toussaint.

Everyone laughed except for Jim. "What do you mean?"

"They have been expecting us," Toussaint said. "Word of our journey was sent ahead when we crossed over into Iraq from Syria."

Then the question that had been nagging Jim since they headed to this destination came out. "So, archeological guys… and woman, what are we going to do now? Do we just knock on the front door and say, "Excuse me, we are here on an important mission to rip up the caves and maybe even the floors of your ancient monastery and take millions of dollars worth of artifacts out of here when we leave?'"

"That is a very good question, Jim," said Larson. "As curious as you are about everything, I'm surprised you haven't already answered it."

"In a way," said Toussaint, "that is exactly what we are going to do, but with the full permission of the monks."

"What? I don't get it."

"You will see, Jim," said Larson as they approached the lower gate of the monastery. The moon had returned from behind the cloud revealing high stone walls in four tiers like half a wedding cake pressed against the side of a steep mountain. Each successive higher wall was less tall and sat within the bigger one below it. As each wall neared the mountainside it clung to, it grew difficult to discern what was man-made, and what was carved directly into the mountain. At random places around the walls were small round towers built with an arched roof, like a minaret jutting into the sky. All of these were lit with lamps of fire and shone brightly into the Iraqi night. It looked as if the inhabitants had fled without turning out the lights because there wasn't one single person in sight.

As if on cue, the doors swung open. Out walked several men dressed in long black robes with high black hats. Their gray beards flowed gracefully down to a long chain that held nothing more than a plain crucifix. They smiled at the travelers. The priest in the front opened his arms wide and greeted them.

"Messier Toussaint...you have returned!"

"I am forever the last one to know anything," thought Jim. Of course, these guys are all over the place. "Why am I surprised?"

"Brother Omar, my dear friend," Toussaint dismounted and embraced the leader. "Please let me introduce you to my companions."

The introductions went around for both sides, with Jim immediately forgetting the complicated and strange names of each monk the moment they pronounced the next one. A group of monks took the horses, but not before Weinberg pulled his saddlebag off of his horse and tossed them over his shoulder. The rest followed the leader into the monastery. In the old city of Jerusalem, he had seen buildings like this, but here in this faraway outpost Jim sensed the primeval nature of the building and all its vestments.

Down a narrow passage lit with candles, they entered a wider main room that split out into three different directions. They hung a left and emerged in a dining hall. Some monks were bringing bowls of food and jars of drink out, placing them on a table near the back of the rows of benches.

"Of course, we've already taken our meals and finished our evening prayers, but we prepared something special for your arrival and planned to serve you whenever you finally arrived," said Omar. "You have made remarkable time getting here and we are glad to welcome you...all of you," he said, looking at Jim with a smile, "and are excited to hear about your news."

"Well, we've much to tell," said Toussaint. "You see, we first discovered this series of scrolls in the home of a wealthy merchant on the Greek island of Akatori and then..."

"Please, have your meal before you begin," said Omar, "you must be very hungry from your journey. Brother Bartholomew, please serve our lady guest first."

"Why thank you so much," said Sara with a lift of her eyebrows to the others for the monk's special treatment.

They settled into a delicious meal of stew and bread, washing it down with pitchers of water and the monk's home made beer. After they were fed, Weinberg, Sara, and Toussaint told the story of the discovery, the double-back trick of Sylvus, and the events that led them to the doors of the monastery.

Weinberg unrolled the map that Avi and Sol had drawn based on the documents they had and Toussaint's memory of the monastery grounds from his previous visit. Omar studied it and the began making the adjustments to the home he'd known since boyhood.

"You see, this place is very, very old. It has been built, destroyed, and rebuilt over centuries of layers of the older structures. When the first monks came here just after the time of Christ, there was nothing here but caves. By the time brother Sylvus had arrived, did you say 47 AD? The construction above these caves had barely begun. Then there were two military destructions and rebuilding of the place."

Larson looked concerned. If a wholesale destruction of the monastery was required, the monks may not be willing to go along with the idea.

Omar studied the hand-drawn map again along with the notes, "However, by your map and my understanding of the way our home is built into the original mountain and cave structure, there are three possibilities for where this Ancient Library could be located," he paused and stroked his beard.

"I am concerned for the relics and sacred things here. There are many old treasures in this monastery. You are not the first to seek the past here. The coffins of the saints of old have been interned for centuries in these walls and in the caves beneath us. Why, they make up the foundation of the four altars in this sacred place. We are reluctant to disturb these sacred relics, and would not do so without great cause. I must tell you that each of the places indicated in the map go through the oldest and most hallowed parts of our sanctuary. To break the stones and dig behind them...well, they will never be the same again. And for us, as you can tell, change comes ever so slowly."

Every monk understood the situation and sat looking with respect at their leader. He was the wisdom and foundation of their order. They would obey his command without reservation.

Weinberg, Sara, Toussaint, Larson, and Jim waited for him to speak again. Jim observed the moment. It was like watching one of those international chess competitions in which both players stared hard at the board, only here no clock was ticking. Finally Omar spoke.

"But this chamber may well contain the autographs of the scriptures, possessions of our Lord, the most sacred of all relics. If these were to be discovered and brought to light...a painting of the Christ..." his voice caught with emotion, "I cannot imagine the power, the majesty, and the way God might use such a discovery in our time."

He looked up with a broad grin, eyes moist. "Let us all get some rest. We will begin in the morning!" The other monks cheered and talked to one another with great excitement.

"Thank you, Omar, for your gracious hospitality," said Toussaint. Each of the Safari Adventure Company members shook his hand and thanked him.

"Whatever it takes to do this great thing, we will support you. All of our resources will be at your service. Time is precious, and we are in an unstable land with war on the horizon. Sylvus brought these priceless items here to protect them from an evil dictator. Now the danger is greater in our own land. We will not rest until we have made the Ancient Library safe again."

Another World

"The monastery has many wings including a church with several altars, a burial site for saints and patriarchs, a library containing very old manuscripts, and more than forty small caves used by monks scattered all over the Alqush mountain," Toussaint shared some of what he had learned of the monastery on his previous visit as the others ate a simple but delicious breakfast of hot grain cereal and bread with sweet jam.

"Do you think they have two-percent available in this goat's milk?" asked Jim. "Maybe I could get a latte, too."

"Yes, Jim," said Weinberg "I noticed they have a Starbucks just off the dining area."

"Some of the caves contain numerous carved writings pertaining to the date of establishment as well as other historical details," Toussaint continued. "The monastery also includes large rooms carved in the mountain stone including this incredible dining room we are sitting in. It is able to hold over 100 monks. This truly amazing eight hundred square foot by fifteen feet high dining room is completely carved inside the mountain. Those small vertical portions - " he pointed to the rough stone areas that ran from floor to ceiling "were left uncarved to act as support beams."

"Bartholomew knows a great deal about the history of this place," Weinberg motioned to the young monk seated next to him. "Tell us, Brother, what you were telling me earlier this morning as we walked outside?"

"You dudes are just not gonna believe what a ripping crib this is," Bartholomew said with a big smile that revealed a bright gold front tooth.

Everyone turned, surprised to hear a surfer-accented "dude" come out of the mouth of an Iraqi monk!

"The monastery was built during the patriarchship of Isho-yab II around 628-644 AD with the assistance of two Ninevite princes. It was like a totally famous attraction here, like the Berkeley of learning and religion especially during the tenth to twelfth centuries."

Then Bartholomew's face became more serious, "That's when, the monastery was attacked, just ripped, man, by hairy smelly Mongols on horseback. They put the place under siege, you know, they like camped all around the place and tried to starve the place out. They got tired of waiting because these monks are like 'chip-monks,' you know what I mean? They had so much stuff stashed in the underground that it was like the monks were doing the siege. The Mongols finally burnt it up and ran them off. The monastic life eventually came back to Dair Rabban Hurmiz a few years after, but on a much smaller scale."

"Bartholomew, where in the world are you from?" asked Weinberg.

"Yeah," said Sara, the language expert.

"Well, dudes and ma'am, I'm from California."

"What are you doing here then?" said Jim.

"Man, it's a totally lengthy tale. If I go back to the cradle and run it down, it could take a tad, you know?"

Everyone laughed. "Okay," said Jim, "give us the short version."

"Well, like, I was this totally loser surfer bum hanging out on Redondo Beach back in the sixties. You all know about the sixties, right?"

"We've heard," said Jim.

"Well, cool, okay then. I was right in the middle of that whole love and peace thing and just hanging out. My friend Lance invited me to this surfer church on the beach and I really started to groove on the whole Jesus thing. I up and got saved, became a Christian, man, it like totally turned my whole head around, if you know what I mean!"

"I know what you mean. Did they call you Bart in California?" asked Weinberg.

"Whoa, that is so freaky, man, yes! But, no one calls me that here. My real name is Bartholomew and that is like a real legendary dude in these parts, so that's what they call me now."

"That is so cool," said Jim, caught up in Bartholomew's excitement.

"I dig it man. Right? So anyway, this group of Jesus freaks like me started organizing a trip over here to help people and I came along. We traveled around a lot in the Middle East staying in hostels and such, and we took the hike and backpacked out here. When I got here I was like so totally buzzed – I thought – this is my home, so I asked to stay. Brother Omar is my language teacher," Bartholomew replied. "He studied in Oxford in England. He believes these cats got to prepare for a new world and that monks will be a big, big link to the world in a new way soon. Omar believes Iraq will open up again to the world and that, as we get nearer the end of the history book, there's gonna be a whole bunch of pilgrims hopping here. And since much of the world speaks English, I'm getting to teach it to the monks.

"And, indeed, here we are!" Weinberg practically shouted and slapped the table with both palms. "Yes," Jim raised his hand, "pilgrim number one, reporting for duty!"

"Please continue, Bartholomew."

Bartholomew recounted the history of the monastery in his colorful way. "In 1722, over 60 monks boogied out of the monastery after the attack by this totally evil guy Nader-Shah, and hid out. Monastic life came back again in 1808. The monastery got going again and continued successfully until the Kurdish uprising in North Iraq between 1963-1974, which caused the monks and Brother Omar, who was the priest even way back then, to vacate the mountain. The Chaldean Church was able to return to the monastery in 1975 and Brother Omar has continued to care for it till today."

Omar approached the table. The Safari Adventure Company members all greeted him and thanked him for his gracious hospitality. The beds were soft and comfortable and the food, though strange to Jim's palate, was tasty and nourishing.

"And a very good morning indeed to you all," Omar welcomed the group. "I overheard my best pupil giving you the history of the monastery. Are you dudes learning a lot from him?"

They all praised the monk's lesson. He beamed a happy smile.

"Toussaint, I've studied the map you brought with the possible locations of the original storage cave. I have considered what might be the most likely one so we may begin our excavation there. I would like to minimize the destruction of this sacred place as much as possible. I'm sure you feel the same way."

"Of course. What have you come to decide?" Toussaint asked.

"The church here contains four altars, The Raban Hurmiz Altar being the oldest and simplest in the monastery. The north and west walls are part of the mountain and the floor is made up of stone coffins. This tiny altar is, in my view, the best site selection of all."

"Are you seriously thinking of busting up the oldest and most sacred altar in the monastery?" Bartholomew asked.

"When I was a young boy, we used to play in the caves around this place. The monks were rebuilding the monastery slowly and we would sneak in to look around when they were at prayers."

"Brother Omar," said Bartholomew with surprise, "you were such a bad boy – look at you now."

"I was not always like totally old, Bartholomew my son." Omar said laughing.

"The church was in very bad condition at that time - holes in the walls and many of the altars badly damaged and crumbled with age. There is a cave behind the Raban Hurmiz Altar that was covered up by the rebuilding. My friends and I explored it many times. It not wide or large; a man can barely squirm through some of its passages. It is however, full of complex passages and goes deep into the mountain.

"Do you think that what we have come to find is there?" Larson said.

"If I were Sylvus searching for someplace to store the most sacred of treasures, then I would have stored them there. I can almost see his form moving along the passageways with the clay jars mentioned in the documents."

"I can't believe we are sitting here talking about this," said Jim to Weinberg.

"I know. It's exciting, isn't it?"

"Well, then, we must get to it, right?" Larson stood, hiked up his belt and rubbed his palms together.

"We have already begun," said Omar standing. "I've had the brothers working in the area since early this morning. Will you join us?"

Jim wiped his mouth and got up quickly from his seat. He followed the group out of the arched doorway of the dining hall and into a passage that led to the church. As they entered the church, Jim was astonished to see gigantic paintings of scenes from the Bible surrounded by intricate art and carvings that seemed to cover every inch of the surprisingly big room.

Each panel was a museum piece. The paintings were very, very old. Some were twenty and thirty feet tall. They looked like ones he had seen in art museums in the United States. Jim recalled a tour guide in Washington DC pointing out how most of the traditional paintings of these Bible scenes were done in the Renaissance period and that the artists put Jesus and the saints in the clothing and scenery of their time. It was true. Some even showed the apostles in the ruffled collars, hose, and pointed shoes of European noblemen. Jim tried to imagine modern artists painting the past in suits and ties, or running shoes and tank tops.

There was Daniel in the lion's den, Moses with the Ten Commandments, the gentle form of Jesus teaching and healing. Finally, the largest painting was of Jesus in agony on a wooden cross with dark stormy clouds gathered all around him. On the ground were the Roman guards gambling for his pathetic robe as well as two reactions to his execution: believers mourning and scoffers laughing. The two thieves on either side of him looked on as if contemplating the dying words they would speak to him. They never knew they would be immortalized in the gospels as eternal testaments to the simplicity of free will faith and rejection of the living truth. In the dark skies, three angels floated weeping, helpless at the terrible price God was paying, sacrificing his only son for the salvation of mankind.

Jim stared at the painting, studying every feature and intricate detail. It must have taken years to complete such a masterpiece. The frame was golden gilded but dull with age. In fact, everything in the place looked like it needed a good dusting and furniture polish.

Someone touched his shoulder. Jim turned to see Bartholomew standing next to him. "That's a major mojo, huh?" he asked. Jim was suddenly aware of the noise and commotion going on at the front of the church and in the room off the pulpit that housed the oldest altar.

"Yes, the fact that something so rare and priceless is hanging in a cave in this desolate area of Northern Iraq boggles the mind."

"No man, I meant the scene, the painting. Look at what is happening. Don't you wonder what it would have been like to have been in the crowd that day?" Bartholomew asked. "Earthquakes, storms, dead people rising out of graves – man, the world changed forever that day."

"Yes," Jim answered. "Yes, it truly is remarkable."

"Yes, it is truly remarkable." Bartholomew mimicked Jim, "that's what you've got to say?"

"Well…"

Just below the mighty work of art was a normal-sized portrait. The painting was extremely old. The years had turned its once-bright colors to a darkening gray and brown, but the image was still clear against the yellowing background. The man in the painting appeared to be about thirty years old. His features were altogether unremarkable, a plain man with reddish hair and a straggly short beard, the sort of person you might pass on the street and never remember having seen. But while the rest of the man was nothing special, the dark eyes were. They seemed to pierce through the centuries, reaching out and grabbing the viewer's attention.

"What is this one?" he asked Bartholomew.

"Unusual attraction, hey?"

"I'll say," Jim replied. "I can't put my finger on it but, yes."

The man in the painting was seated on rock and facing a group of people he might have been addressing, their backs turned to the painter.

"Looks a lot like a photograph of someone caught by a camera in the middle of giving a talk, doesn't it? More like a photograph."

"Yes. Yes it does.

"Well, Big Jim, the monastery keeps a highly detailed record of every work of antiquity, art, and decoration in this place. All of these paintings, tapestries, and vestments are identified by the dates they were acquired and how they got here. This place may seem like totally random and all, but in reality, the monks before us and right up to this day, only move or restore or relocate or...heaven forbid...as a last resort, destroy any of these relics.

"I can answer for you or look up the answer, for all of these. That is of course..."

"Except for this painting," Jim interrupted.

"Bingo Jim," the monk touched the frame carefully. "Oh...this one is my personal favorite picture. Brother Omar brought me to see it after I'd lived here about half a year. I was really starting to love the monastery and the brothers. I had not felt love for anyone in so long. This painting brought out the yearning and pain I felt for my parents and sisters who had died when I was only a little dude.

"Brother Omar brought you to this painting?"

"Yes, he brought me here. We sat on that bench," he motioned to a small wooden bench that faced the painting, "and asked me to consider the teacher in this painting. Like you, I could not stop staring at the eyes of the teacher. He seemed to comfort me in a way I can't say, even now."

"I didn't tell you I was drawn to the eyes," Jim said, a bit embarrassed.

"But you totally were, man. I look for it whenever I show someone this painting. You found the painting on your own, and I checked you out as you looked at it. Your pupils got massive when you looked into the face."

"So what DO you know about this picture, then?"

"If you follow the records back from modern times, it keeps getting moved around, always referred to as The Teacher. The earliest records only mention it was brought here from the caves occupied by the first monks, the ones who came from Turkey, before even the monastery itself was built."

"Really? So it is very old, then?"

"Yeah, old, older, oldest. The archaeologists and scientists who come here haven't paid much attention to it; it is so plain and simple amongst these big-dog paintings and all. Everyone who has examined it, plus all the monks and most importantly Brother Omar, say its the oldest thing in the entire monastery."

"Jim, come here!" Larson shouted from across the room.

They turned and moved toward the area where all the noise was coming from. Jim had to duck his head to get through the low narrow stone entrance. The Raban Hurmiz Altar was ancient indeed. The simple carved portico was at once beautiful and plain. Two sides of the room were carved into the rock of the mountain. The other two walls were simple stone blocks. A battery-powered lantern had been moved into the room washing the ancient walls in bright light. The monks had obviously been digging for a while and had made great progress already.

Using crowbars and simple hand tools, they had removed four of the stone coffins. With a brilliantly clever system of pulleys and ropes they had lifted each one and hauled them out into the main church area where they now sat carefully placed in reverence in front of the pulpit.

In the hole left by the coffins was a man covered with dirt. He would bend down for a moment and then stand up again, straining to lift a basket full of dirt to a monk by the opening who would then hand it fire-brigade style to another. These baskets were handed to a series of monks who transferred them to others who carried them out to a growing pile in the main hall.

Omar stood talking to Toussaint by the opening. He pointed and said, "there are four other men already in the tunnel below. Two of them have picks and digging tools. They tell me that they have removed much of the dirt and broken through the first of the stones that form the wall sealing the cave behind it."

"Are you serious?" asked Larson. "I thought this was going to take days."

"It may take long time to find your scroll," said the monk in the hole, his bright eyes shown through a dirt and sweat streaked face as he lifted another bucket "But you will walk in this cave today."

Into the Darkness

While the monks completed their work opening up the cave behind the altar, Toussaint, Larson, and Sara returned to the horses and unpacked the archaeological excavation equipment they had brought along. They opened the heavy packs and took an inventory of all the supplies they had. Should they discover the artifacts, preserving them and protecting them as fast as possible would be critical. Digital cameras were readied along with the storage disks they would use to document the find. Notebooks and tiny digital voice recorders were checked for battery power and reliability.

Jim and Weinberg walked past the hallway to the dining room with Bartholomew as their tour guide. They could hear the others talking excitedly about the project. The archaeologists had waited a long time and survived nearly fatal attacks. Now they were on the adventurer's second highest peak...the brink of discovery!

Outside the monastery, Bartholomew gave Jim and Weinberg the tour of the systems that supported the monks and their simple existence. There were small stables and low barns with healthy horses, goats, llamas, chickens and a few cows. These were surrounded by patches of hand-tended gardens squeezed anywhere the rocky land yielded a few meters of tillable soil.

Though brother Omar had invested many of the monks in the task of opening the altar, still some moved along the paths to and from the tasks that made the system work.

Bartholomew was a fountain of information and seemed genuinely thrilled to have an English-speaking audience. They re-entered the monastery and made their way to the final area of the tour Jim broke the pattern and asked questions about his work. "Why are you a monk?" he began.

"Well, the original monks like the Essene sect of Judaism wanted to get out of the social pollution and heathenism of the cities and the feudal systems that governed them. They sought these totally remote locations and structured their lives so they could focus on the pursuit of Godliness, holiness, prayer, and study," he began a rehearsed explanation.

"No," said Jim, "Why did *you* become a monk?'

"I could tell you about growing up an orphan. Or I could tell you how I was treated well by the Christian priest in a village about 100 kilometers from here. I could even say that the cruelty I saw in the cities I worked in as a teenager just blew me away. But in the end, I suppose I came to this place for many of the same reasons the very first monks came. I wanted to make something different of my life than the endless pursuit of possessions and money, and to become one, a vessel if you will, that could be used by God for His purpose."

"Wow," said Jim.

"You have made a wise choice with your life, Bartholomew," said Weinberg. "You are an excellent monk and a bright student."

"Right on, Weinberg!" Bartholomew "high-fived" the Englishman.

"I believe your desire to be used useful to God in a special way will indeed be accomplished. Perhaps even sooner than you think."

"Whoa, a prophet you are, then, Sir?" The young monk asked.

"No prophet," Weinberg smiled, "but an enlightened optimist."

"Here we are now, the final part of the tour. This…" he said opening a wide wooden door into a circular room, "is one of the baddest libraries you will ever see."

The room was filled from floor to ceiling with books and papers. They ranged in age and condition from brand new to hundreds of years old. "This is truly amazing," said Weinberg running from shelf to shelf, unable to decide what to look at first. He settled on a sagging shelf of ancient-looking texts and began scrutinizing the lot.

"Look, Jim!" Weinberg pointed to a green book with gold letters. "The Safari Chronicles, Volume 1…one of the original hardcovers!"

"Is it signed?" Asked Jim.

"Sure is," Weinberg examined the first page. "This book really gets around, huh? Oh, for heaven's sake. Here's another treasure! May I?" he asked with his hand over a faded book.

"Yes, you may open and read any of these," said Bartholomew. "It is scarcity city on English texts, I'm afraid. I could use more in my studying. In fact many are in Greek and Latin. The very oldest are not even bound books but some amazing manuscripts and scrolls."

"You have manuscripts here?" Jim said.

"Yes, our oldest are of the scriptures themselves and date back to the second century," Bartholomew stated in a matter-of-fact voice.

"No!" Weinberg practically shouted. "Does Toussaint know this?"

"Oui, Messier," said Toussaint stepping in through the open door with Sara. "He knows and has seen them!"

"You are kidding me, Toussaint," said Weinberg, eyes wide. "That would mean manuscripts copied from the originals. I've never seen such an old copy. Where are they?"

"Lady and gentlemen, right through this door." Bartholomew motioned to a door at the back of the room. "You can see for yourselves."

"Come on!" said Sara as she led the way.

The room was smaller. The walls were lined not with open bookshelves, but with glass cases and sealed drawers designed to protect the most ancient and sacred artifacts. Along one wall was an angled case displaying sections of an unrolled manuscript in the stylish inked calligraphy of the most ancient writing style on a yellowed and delicate parchment. Bartholomew lit lamps on each side of the case. The warm light cast just the right illumination on the scroll.

"A second-century manuscript. It's worth millions and they don't even lock the door." Jim came closer and looked at the scroll. Something fresh and magical came over him as he looked at the half-familiar Greek letters that formed the words he could not understand.

"Is it accurate to what the Bibles of today say? Or are there lots of differences?" asked Jim.

Bartholomew smiled and nodded yes. "Dude, that is like the first question asked by almost everybody who comes in here. You don't have to take my word for it, though. Can anyone here read second-century Greek?"

"Dr. Sara Einstein," said Toussaint, "I believe this is your specialty."

Sara stepped closer to the glass case and peered into the manuscript. She took a moment to get her mental footing, adjusting to the writing style and era of the language. She then began in a quiet but strong voice.

"While Jesus was still speaking, they came from the house of Jairus, the synagogue leader, saying, 'Your daughter has died; why trouble the Teacher anymore?' But Jesus, overhearing what was spoken, said to the synagogue official, 'Do not be afraid, just keep on believing.'

"And He allowed no one to follow with Him, except Peter and James and John the brother of James.

"And they came to the house of the synagogue official; and He beheld a commotion and loud wailing weeping and wailing.

"And entering in, He said to them, 'Why make a commotion and weep. The child has not died, but is asleep.'

"And they began laughing at him. But putting them all out, He took along the child's father and mother and His own companions, and entered where the child was."

Sara's eyes moved to the next manuscript in the case. "Could you please angle that lamp better so I can see this one?" Bartholomew did so.

She began again at the top of the next manuscript scroll.

"And taking the child by the hand, He said to her, ('Talitha kum' which means 'Little girl, I say to you, arise!')

"And immediately the girl rose to walk; for she was twelve years old." Weinberg's voice boomed out across the room, startling Jim and stopping Sara, "And immediately they were completely astounded."

Everyone turned to look at Weinberg who continued to recite from memory, eyes closed. "And He gave them strict orders that no one should know about this; and He said that something should be given to her to eat," he paused and opened his eyes. "Luke Chapter 5, if I am correct."

"The Gospel of St. Luke Chapter 5 verses 35-43, you are correct Mr. Weinberg," said Bartholomew.

"I thought that Jesus put on a big show everywhere he went to get as many people as possible to believe the miracles he was doing. What's up with him ordering the people who saw him actually raise someone from the dead not to tell anyone? Wouldn't that be a clincher in any town?" asked Jim.

"Well," said Sara, "Jesus had a public ministry for sure. But what we see throughout all four of the Gospels is that he often did things for just the private audience of his disciples."

"And almost always after a public miracle he took them away to a private place," said Weinberg, "and explained the deeper meaning of his actions – and how they consistently reflected complete harmony, an explanation or revealing, of the word of God as written in the Jewish scriptures or Christian Old Testament."

"Not exactly Benny Hinn putting on a big show in a sports arena in front of television cameras then, was he?" said Jim, referring to a glitzy televangelist he'd seen while channel surfing back home.

"Not even Benny has pretended to raise someone from the dead, has he?" asked Weinberg. Larson shrugged his shoulders. Jim looked at the manuscript and thought about the story. Everything about this place seemed a long way from a television studio.

"The primary *function* of teaching the Apostles was to prepare them to launch the church and write the scriptures that would be the presence of Jesus throughout the ages," said Sara. "Jesus was one man, in one place in time; the Word and the church were portable and reproducible. By pouring his life into these twelve men, he set in motion a chain of events that continues to this day."

Jim thought about Sara using the word function, and how the rabbi in Jerusalem had taught him to use the function – the "what does it do" question – to understand Hebraic thought. When you looked at this story in that light, Sara was right. His purpose was to teach the apostles, who would teach the world when the story was complete.

They examined the other sights of the room for a while, then, one by one, left the archives. Weinberg went back to the main library room, leaving Jim and Bartholomew alone.

"You cannot imagine how incredibly…" he wanted to say cool, but thought there had to be a more dignified word, "…*wonderful*, it is that you live in this place, among such historical reality and amazing treasure."

"Hey, I am one lucky amigo, for many reasons," Bartholomew agreed. "Living with these amazing monks is awesome. I really dig the work and the study is something you won't get at community college in L.A. Maybe I've been here long enough that I kind of take some of this for granted. I hope not. But, hey Jim, you know that the Bible you buy in a bookstore is just as rare and precious."

"What do you mean?"

"Don't you see, man? The *words* are the same. Jesus spoke them and so did his apostles. They knew who he really was, they faithfully recorded exactly what he said in public and to them privately. It's the *words* that are alive still today."

"You really believe that, don't you?" Jim said.

"*Of course I believe* what is undeniably true. This manuscript is proof that the scriptures are functionally identical as far back as one thousand nine hundred years. That's during the lifetimes of eyewitnesses of Jesus when he was still alive! They survived persecution, banning, destruction, the dark ages, plagues, and attacks from every direction. Some people will come to this place and see this copy of the original autograph of the words of our Lord. They dig that what they have is the most carefully and accurately preserved and the most right-on written work of antiquity on the planet."

Bartholomew lowered his voice, which had begun to rise. "And they will be historically convinced of the reliability of the Bible they read today. This is a great comfort to them. But the true test of the accuracy of these words is to trust them, pursue, and dive deeply into the understanding of them as an entire work, not some snippet of a story. Live by them and THEN you will see the results."

"Do you think Jesus actually spoke these exact words?" Jim said.

"Let me ask you a question, Jim." Bartholomew squared up and faced Jim directly. "If you had spent a year with the most incredible human being who ever lived, watched His astonishing miracles, ate with him, got thirsty and bummed out and traveled miles of dusty roads with him; if you had seen him handle fierce persecution and endless testing from the religious leaders of the day and found him to be the most consistent, wisest, sinless and perfect person you'd ever encountered," the monk pointed his finger back at the manuscript case and held it there, "and he looked you in the eye and said, Jim buddy, you come with me. I want you to see this. And then you followed him from a crowded public speech to a house where people were mourning the death of a twelve-year-old little girl…and he brought that dead girl back to life," he caught his breath.

"Man, do you think you just might remember that exact moment with clarity?"

"Well, sure, but…"

"And do you think that, years later, after he came back from the dead himself and chose you to write it all down, and supernaturally empowered you to do it … do you think that it is at least *possible* you would remember what he said?"

"Yes, I could see how that could happen."

"Then you are well on your way to believing that it really did happen, just as millions and millions of other people believe. Not from laying their mitts on an old piece of old paper, but by placing their hearts, their hands and most of all their minds in the care of the words of life.

"So you believe he spoke those exact words," Jim asked again.

Bartholomew rolled his eyes and sighed, "Hey dude, pay attention, eyes on me, mouth closed.... Jesus spoke those precise words. On that exact day, in that real town, he used words to bring life to the little girl, to her mother and father, to the apostles who were there, and about ten minutes ago, he spoke them to you. They came out of the mouth of Dr. Einstein, but just as sure as we are standing here, He spoke them to you."

Archaeologists

Equipped with battery-powered lanterns attached to sturdy plastic helmets, the members of the Safari Adventure Company stepped one by one into the opening near the altar where the stone coffins had been removed. The excavation had taken a lot longer than Brother Omar had predicted. A second shift replaced the first one as attempts to break through the wall had become a much more difficult project than they'd first imagined.

As the work went on into the night, Larson had recommended they get some sleep and begin in the morning, fresh and ready. It had been a good suggestion. As the day wore on, the fatigue of the journey on horseback overcame the anticipation of the adventure ahead. They were all fast asleep in their cells soon after the evening meal.

Now the dawn was breaking outside the monastery behind the mountain that held it. They washed in basins of water warmed by the kitchen fire and hurried breakfast. They stepped down onto the wooden steps placed inside the opening and moved through another opening in the wall. Jim saw right away why it had taken so long to clear a tunnel. Except for a small opening near the top of the first wall, the rest was made up of three sections of large stones stacked irregularly into interlocking pieces. They required the removal of a huge section to get all the way through. Thankfully, they had been spared this labor, he thought.

Larson led the way, followed closely by Toussaint, Sara, Weinberg, and finally Jim. Once inside the wall, they huddled around the map they had studied the day before and first thing in this morning.

"Omar says this is a big place, with lots of tunnels. We want to make the best use of the people we have here, so this is the plan." Larson unrolled the map highlighted in different colors. "We break up into groups of two and search these sections here. This should take about an hour apiece, then we return here, report in, make sure everyone is okay, and make our plan for the next sweep."

"Sounds good to me," said Weinberg. "Who's paired up?"

"Sara, you can come with me; Toussaint, you and Jim go down this way, and Weinberg, you go with Bartholomew."

A pair of faded Nike running shoes plopped down into the opening beyond the wall behind them. Seconds later, Bartholomew's lantern headlight appeared through the wall and he walked into the group.

"Good morning, Bartholomew!" Weinberg called out. You, my friend, will be in charge of tiny openings and difficult spots today. I see you are dressed for just such a thing."

The headlights of the group turned to illuminate a man with long hair sticking out of a hardhat wearing jeans and a tie-dyed T-shirt instead of his black robe. "This feels totally odd indeed," he said smiling. "It's been a while, you know?"

Larson handed everyone a small plastic referee's whistle. "If anyone should find what you believe to be the location, check it out carefully and then return to the meeting place and blow this whistle. We should be able to hear it in all the tunnels we are searching at this point. We will return here and go together to work it," he insisted.

"If you get in trouble or get hurt, stay calm, but blow the whistle periodically and we will hear you from the meeting place and come to your assistance. There shouldn't be any big danger down here, but anything is possible. Go slow. Take your time. See you back here in an hour.

"Bartholomew, do you have any questions?"

"Blow the whistle for good, blow the whistle for bad, or don't blow the whistle at all."

"Very good!" Larson laughed along with the others as he looked at the beaming faces around him. He could not imagine being any more excited than this. "Okay, then, off we go."

Toussaint led the way as Jim followed. They moved carefully through the labyrinth of the cave, making notes and shining their lanterns down the numerous side corridors. Some of these held enough promise that they marked their location and pursued the tunnel, only to find it grew smaller and smaller until it reached a dead end.

Two times, they returned to the meeting area to find that the others had an identical experience and had returned empty-handed. On the third time, Jim could hear Larson and Sara talking with great excitement to Weinberg and Bartholomew. When they reached the group, they were looking at a large section of pottery and a short metal sword, the handle withered but still wrapped tightly around the bottom.

She and Larson had found the pottery between two rocks, the sword nearby. Sara identified the pottery as First-Century Roman. Toussaint examined it and concurred. The section of cave they had found the items in was too long to check completely in the hour they had allotted themselves. They consulted the map and planned for all three groups to explore the tunnels in and around the new area that had produced results.

"We might be down here for days, we'd better get some lunch," suggested Larson. Jim didn't want to stop searching, especially since they'd found something that seemed to be almost a big sign pointing THIS WAY TO THE TREASURE! But he understood the approach of the professionals, and besides, he was getting hungry.

They let him carry the sword back to the top.

"Are you going to eat with that thing?" Weinberg joked as Jim showed his big treasure to all the monks within shouting distance. "Oh, come on, I'm really excited," said Jim as he tore into his food and ate too fast.

"Yes, I suppose you are. So am I, Jim." Weinberg grinned from ear to ear and gave his thumbs-up sign.

They went back into the caves with full water bottles and renewed excitement. Larson had them all check their watches. Each moved out into his or her reassigned area with eyes wide open. Jim and Toussaint talked of the Frenchman's past digs and adventures. His respect for the European archaeologist was already high. In spite of their obvious differences, they had something important in common. Both had faced the evil Kalil and had lived to tell about it. The stitches where Kalil's knife had sliced a big chunk off the Frenchman's ear had only been out a couple of days when they left for Iraq.

About twenty minutes into their search, conversation ceased. The cave grew narrower and then wider while the ceiling ran high overhead, then painfully short. At this point, it had gotten so low, they had to proceed slowly on all fours. Toussaint stopped, turned sideways, and wriggled through a narrow passage. Jim was left alone for a moment on the other side. He eyed the slit in the craggy rock and paused to see if the Frenchman would discover a dead end and save him the trouble of squeezing his six-foot-two-inch body into that keyhole.

In the darkness, he took a moment to reflect. So many things had to go just so for him to be here. Had Sara's father not figured out where to find them, he would have probably died in the torture chamber in Libya. For that matter he could well have died in the blast at the hotel. Toussaint, too, had danced with fate when Kalil had chosen to sever a piece of his ear rather than stab or shoot him on the beach. Jim wondered where Kalil was right now. Could he be in Turkey excavating in vain some section of that Underground City? Thank goodness he wasn't clued into their location now. He closed his eyes and hoped he'd never see the cold evil eyes of Kalil again.

"Toussaint, are you okay in there?" Jim called into the distance ahead.

"Yes, yes, Jim, thank you. I am in a larger room with several passages out. Don't bother to squeeze in here just yet until I see if these are just dead ends or something more, okay?

"You got it," Jim agreed. He lay down on his side sending his helmet light into the side of the corridor. Although the ceiling was flat, the corridor was wide to the right. His eye caught a glimmer of metal. He moved his light again and several more bits of metal reflection shone back at him. It appeared that a section of rock had collapsed revealing a chamber that had been obscured. Jim scooted toward it.

A few moments later, he laid his hand on something cold, metallic, and definitely manmade. He tried to pull it up, but it produced a sound like the piercing scraping noise made by a car when its brakes need replaced. In his confined position, though, it would not come loose. It seemed to be held by whatever other metal was piled around it. From his new vantage point, Jim shone the light back into what looked like a stack of iron tools and broken pottery. The pattern on the pottery resembled the piece Sara had brought back from the last search. Jim's heart leaped in his chest...his first archaeological find! His thoughts rushed a million miles an hour imagining what ancient hands had touched these items last. His heart beat rapidly in his ears. He called out to Toussaint, "Hey I think you'd better get back out here real quick!"

There was no answer from the opening. "Toussaint?" Jim called again louder. Still, there was silence. Jim wriggled away from the artifacts and crawled on his hands and knees to the opening. He raised himself up and peered inside. Sure enough, just as Toussaint had reported, the room opened up a good bit, and then led off in four or five different directions. The Frenchman would know what to do about the things he had found. He had to tell him. He drew a breath and cupped his hands to shout Toussaint's name as loud as he could. Just as he was about to call out, Jim heard the distant shrill blast of the whistle coming from one of the tunnels off the main room inside.

"Toussaint," Jim yelled as loud as he could, "are you hurt?"

War Machines

"You, listen up!" The commander kicked the bottom of the boot of the nearest soldier. He had drifted almost to sleep as he lie in the ground listening to the leader go over the plan again. "Let's go over this one more time. Only this time you sit up and listen. Knowing what to do without having to think about what to do could save your life, Mahkesh. Do you understand this?"

"Yes, sir. I'm sorry." The soldier sat up straighter and rotated his shoulders to get his blood circulating. The commander gave him his best frown, but they both knew he wouldn't discipline him any further than a stern reprimand. After all, they were all volunteers and the "soldiering" they did was all guerilla sting-and-hide work anyway. Guiding troops like these was a delicate balance between good old military discipline and paternal sports coaching.

"Very well. We have a two-hour ride around the valley in the trucks. When we arrive at the drop point, we will load our gear and march to here." He pointed to a red mark on the worn map. "Then we will set up a line-of-sight launch area and wait for their supply trucks to come up the road from the South. When the..." the commander stopped talking and looked up into the sky to the Northwest.

All fourteen soldiers looked up as soon as he did, some twisting around so they could see into the direction where the barely perceptible sound came from. The sound got louder fast. "They are traveling at top speed - *CONCEAL*!" shouted the leader to the men who were already scrambling for the cover of the trees.

Within seconds, the roar of battle-ready aircraft that should have been too heavy to fly tore across the campsite too low for radar to pick up. The commander of the Kurdish rebels spoke to Samamgi as he watched the machines cross the ridge ahead and bank into the valley beyond. "Well, my sharp-shooting friend. A new mission has just fallen into our laps."

Discovery

Jim waited and listened for a reply from the dark chamber beyond. He cupped his hands and drew a breath to shout again, "Toussaint! Are you…"

"No – no – no. I am fine! I've found it Jim! I've found it!" Toussaint reappeared into the main room almost running. His face filled the hole in the stone as Jim rocked back on his hands and knees to keep from bumping heads. "I blew the whistle because I was so excited, I could not speak. It has to be it! It has to be the Library! Just inside that passage right there." He jerked his thumb over his shoulder without looking behind him. "Just a few steps down that passageway there…the first one I looked in…there are stones piled against the opening but one has fallen from the top! I shone my light inside and looked! It is filled with pottery…all sizes…all completely sealed…intact! It's here, Jim! Do you hear me? The greatest discovery of the history of archaeological history…of the history of the world…of all times…it's sitting right here!"

Jim was shouting back but he didn't know what words he said. Both men were whooping and celebrating like little kids who'd won a carnival prize. "Let me come in and see, then we'll go tell the others right away, okay?" said Jim.

"Sure, sure, come on in. Take that once-in-a-lifetime peek into a sight that no one has seen in two thousand years! Oh my goodness, yes, come on in."

Jim shifted his weight to lean into the opening.

At that moment, they heard the distant but unmistakable sound of one of the other whistles blowing fast and hard, over and over. Every blast sent shivers down his back. What could this mean? If Toussaint was right, the storage cave had already been found. He remembered Bartholomew's words as they began, "Blow the whistle for good, blow the whistle for bad, or don't blow the whistle at all!"

Somewhere, someone was in big, big trouble.

The whistle continued to blast again and again as Toussaint came through the opening. Both he and Jim rushed back to entrance at the altar.

Three Black Helicopters

Over Toussaint's shoulder, Jim could see two figures, perhaps Bartholomew and Weinberg, slipping through the stone wall and heading toward the entrance as they reached the meeting point. The whistle never stopped the entire time they moved toward the altar. There was shouting and confusion and the sound of rushing footsteps above them as they moved into the entrance.

"Three black helicopters are hovering in front of the monastery!" one of the monks shouted to Larson at the top of the entrance. Toussaint and Jim were the last to arrive. "There is a loud voice calling down from the helicopters – Brother Omar is there now. He asked that we bring you as soon as possible – they are asking for you."

"Kalil," said Larson. "He has a network of spies everywhere. I was afraid he might find us here."

"We came in here as carefully and quietly as we could, Larson," Weinberg said. "We've done the best we can to rescue the Library. It may still be here, Larson. What else were we to do?"

"It is not *maybe* here…" Toussaint spoke up. He and Jim were still breathless from hurrying to the front. "It IS here!" The others turned toward the two of them. Toussaint was bent over with his hands on his knees catching his breath. Jim nodded a "yes" to the group.

"You found the Library?" shouted Weinberg and Sara at the same time.

"Yes. It has to be so," Toussaint said. "It's behind a wall of stones like the ones at this entrance. Only, one had fallen out of place. I just had time to look in to the chamber and see, but there are lines of sealed jars. It is just as Sylvus told us it would be. It is perfection!"

"Just outside of the area where he found the wall, I found a stash of metal pieces that I think might have been tools or equipment used to get the stuff down into the cave," said Jim. "There was pottery there that looked like what you brought out before lunch, Sara."

"Oh my...oh my." Sara was excited. "I want to run to the chamber right now!" she said.

"Please, come with me to Brother Omar's assistance. The men in the helicopter are threatening to destroy the monastery. Their helicopters look more powerful than the ones of the Iraqi army. Please hurry!"

"Larson, what are we going to do?" Weinberg asked. "I'm all for a great plan but if Kalil gets access to this place, the artifacts are lost, perhaps destroyed and gone for all time. We can't let him in here."

"Okay, we'll think of something. Sara, you stay here with Bartholomew and watch the entrance," Larson commanded.

"There is no way I'm staying here. You can't just..."

An explosion rocked the chamber. The deep rumbling of an attack on the monastery was felt throughout the mountain structure. As the Safari Adventure Company team ran from the altar chamber in to the larger church, paintings and decorations were falling from the walls. Chiseled into a mountain as it was, there had been few events powerful enough to shake the foundation of the old structure. Now, pews tumbled down and lamps fell to the floor, the fuel inside starting little smoky fires. The monks appeared from every direction rushing buckets of water to extinguish the flames and protecting what they could from further damage.

"Let's go," Larson called over his shoulder as he ran from the church toward the dining hall and the foyer. The others followed as fast as they could. When they reached the entrance, Omar was running in.

"Thank you for interrupting your search and coming up here now, my friends." He was shaken but determined. "They arrived just a while ago and demanded I produce you, Larson, and whomever was in your company. I told them you were not here. They gave me an impossible deadline or they would fire a missile into the monastery."

"Is that what just happened?" said Weinberg.

"Yes, it was horrible. The missile hit the structure somewhere above us and debris went everywhere. We were standing out front. I've sent people to check on the others. I have no idea what kind of damage has been done here.

"Brother Omar, two monks were in the study right above where the missile hit," a bald monk with wire rim glasses ran up to the old priest and reported. "Brothers Samuel and Ali."

"Yes, go on."

"Ali is dead, Omar. He's dead!"

"And Samuel?"

"He's hurt. I don't know how badly. There was blood on his face. What do you want us to do, Brother?"

"Is anyone else hurt?"

"No. Part of the wall is broken in and the whole area is open now."

Without a moment's hesitation, the priest gave his orders. "Move everyone to the church. It is the deepest part of the monastery. He can shoot every missile he has and we will be safer there than anywhere else in the monastery."

"But Brother Omar, what if we abandon this place and flee to the caves around us?"

"I'm afraid that if we get out where the helicopters can see us we are in worse danger."

"He's right," Larson said. He was standing in the doorway looking outside at the attackers. "If you try to run now, the machine guns on these helicopters will kill many of you. At this point, you will be safest inside the mountain."

"Yes, go quickly now and tell everyone," said Omar, waving his hands for the monk to leave.

"Yes, Brother." He turned and ran inside.

Jim stepped up beside Larson and looked out at the deadly force. The black Apache helicopters were hovering in formation three abreast in the sky directly ahead of the mountain entrance of the stone fortress. They seemed so close, but yet far enough from the structure that he could not make out any faces inside. Looking up at the monastery behind him, he could see dark smoke billowing up into the sky.

A voice came over a loudspeaker from one of the helicopters that Jim would never forget. "Priest! You told me Larson and his people are not here. I don't believe you. My sources tell me he is inside with four other companions," Kalil spoke in his icy tone. But unlike the voice in the torture chamber, this time he was audibly furious. "Each of these aircraft has a total of sixteen missiles just like the one we've already fired into your building."

"Good, going Brother Omar!" said Bartholomew.

"The monastery has been a sanctuary to protect good from evil for a very long time," said Omar, placing his hand on the shoulder of his pupil. "We will always do exactly what we believe is right. Always."

Kalil's voice continued to ring down from the sky. "I will fire one of these missiles every five minutes until you produce the Safari Adventure Company people you have inside your building right here in this courtyard."

The helicopter on the far right broke formation at once and took a position directly facing the largest of the barns on the hillside. In a moment's notice, the hissing sound of the missile launched pierced the air. At this distance it moved so fast into its target that Jim wasn't sure he even saw it at all. The deadly projectile slammed into the roof of the barn and into the rocky ground below shattering the structure with a hideous thudding explosion he could feel in his feet. The barn incinerated in a sphere of flame. Smoke billowed up from naked rock where the barn, supplies, feed, tools, and more than two dozen animals were once housed.

Everyone at the entrance shouted in stunned surprise. They stepped back as the vacuum created by the explosion sucked the air past the door of the monastery tearing at their hair in a burst of wind. Larson shouted his anger at Kalil.

"So much for five minutes," said Jim.

Omar turned to the Safari Adventure Company members and said, "I will not sacrifice your lives this way."

"Omar, we cannot let you risk your monks and this sacred place..." Toussaint began.

"Please Toussaint. I believe I understand this situation as well as you. If this terrorist gets you to surrender he will take us all hostage anyway. He will capture you. He will get you to help him find the Library or torture you to death to get what you know. The entrance we've uncovered has already been opened; it's obvious what we are doing in that cave."

Larson stared out at the sky tugging the maroon baseball cap off his head, his rage boiling. Toussaint and Weinberg nodded. Sara and Jim listened.

"If he gets in here now, he will search for the Library until it is found...if it is indeed here."

"It is here, Omar," Toussaint said. "We had just come upon it when the monks began blowing the whistles for us to come back up here."

"Oh, my dear Lord. Then it's really true? The things of Christ have been here in this place for almost two thousand years?"

"We do not know yet what exactly is in the chamber," said the scientist, "but the chamber is intact and filled with sealed jars. I have seen into the chamber with my own eyes."

Omar drew himself up tall. The resolve in his eyes was unmistakable. "If this evil person gets in here, he will steal or destroy these sacred things. My friends, we cannot let this thing happen."

"What do you intend to do, then?" asked Sara. "If we don't do something he will blast how many missiles into here? Three times sixteen is forty-eight warheads. He's only fired two and you've seen what destructive power they have!" The grass and crops near the empty place where the barn had been now caught fire and began to burn behind them.

Forty-six missiles may not annihilate this monastery, but it will bury the site in tons of rubble. If this happens, Kalil will not be able to remain here and perform an excavation. The Iraqi army will descend upon this place when word gets out that there was a battle and missiles fired here. I would be surprised to find that the Kurdish rebel militia hasn't already begun to move here expecting to find some military operation they can ambush.

Jim looked at Sara. "I can't believe this is happening to us," he said. "One minute we are in the midst of this great historical discovery and the next we are in a no-win situation."

"I know," said Sara. "We cannot surrender and we cannot fight. If we take refuge in the church, which it looks like we are going to do, we will probably die anyway. But, at least we will not allow the Library to fall into the hands of Kalil."

"If we go back into the caves, maybe we can at least open the jars and see what is inside while we are there." Jim said.

"No," Toussaint said. "Opening the jars, if we cannot preserve and protect and document the contents, would only risk them being damaged before they are found again."

"If..." added Weinberg, "we do not escape our hiding place."

"I believe we should move inside to the church. There, we can pray and hope this maniac realizes that destroying this place will prevent him from getting what he wants. "If it looks like we need to, we can even go down into the caves below," Omar said. "We have plenty of water and plenty of food. There we will do our best to survive, perhaps find a way out through the caves. This monastery has been completely destroyed two other times in its history, but yet, here it stands. The martyrs who have shed their blood here fought against evil and so shall we. If we are buried alive in this place...even if we die...we will still protect the treasures where they lie, and believe that it is meant for them to come to light in another way...in another time...in God's own good time."

Turning around, Larson said, "Maybe there is one more thing we can try."

It Can't Work

"If you have an idea you'd better get to it fast," demanded Weinberg.

"Do you have any weapons here, Omar? Anything at all?"

"We have a few rifles, a little ammunition for protection from bandits and robbers. We have nothing to attack a military aircraft."

"Where are these guns and ammo?"

"You have four minutes until the next missile is fired," Kalil's voice boomed from the sky. "I am not a patient man and do not know if I can even wait that long."

"How will you get a shot at these things?" Omar asked Larson. "And if you do attempt to shoot at one of them, the others will kill you, then destroy the monastery anyway."

"Omar, please just show Weinberg and Toussaint where the guns are. Weinberg, you two get the weapons and bring them to the dining hall. Jim, you and Bartholomew stay here. I've got a plan." With that, he grabbed Sara by the arm and ran out the front door in plain sight of the helicopters. Omar rushed away with Weinberg and Toussaint. Jim watched from the doorway as Larson ran out to the open courtyard and signaled with his hat. The center helicopter pulled forward slowly from where they had retreated to wait to fire again. It floated closer and closer until the pilot must have been able to see Larson's and Sara's faces clearly.

Larson made the gesture of talking on a telephone then motioned them to come closer several times. A uniform-sleeved hand appeared at the door of the helicopter and tossed down a green canvas knapsack. Larson ran to pick it up and pulled out a small hand-held radio. Sara's short black hair and khaki shirt rippled in the strong wind as Larson returned to her side. He flipped on the radio and shouted into it. Jim could not make out what he was saying, but apparently he was negotiating some kind of a deal. Sara and Larson ran back to the doorway of the monastery.

"What in the world are you *doing*?" Jim shouted as Larson and Sara burst through it,

"Okay, here's the deal," Larson flipped off the power button on the radio then spoke fast. "I bought us about ten minutes but we have to move quickly if this is going to work. I told Kalil that the rest of the team was still down in the excavation area. I told him we hadn't found anything yet. He doesn't believe we haven't found anything but he is giving me ten minutes to get the rest of you out here."

"Well what kind of a plan is that?" asked Jim. "I thought we weren't going to surrender? If we do that, he is going to get everything and probably kill these monks and us, too."

"Look, I told him there were only four of us. He's expecting to see me and Sara and Weinberg and Toussaint walking out in front of this monastery in a few minutes. I will be in that tower we saw on the way in, with a rifle." Larson took Sara's arm and pulled her close to him. He hugged her. "He is going to want to take us all hostage and that means landing the helicopters. As they draw in close enough, I am going to shoot the pilots. It's hot outside, all the windows and doors are open, and they will not be expecting anything like this."

"Oh, my God, Larson," said Sara. "Can you really do this? Can you really take out three attack helicopters with a rifle?" She squeezed his hand.

"I brought down two in Kuwait during Desert Storm. Once I get the first two, the third should be easy." Larson smiled a broad, confident smile that Sara and Jim knew was meant to inspire them more than reveal his real feelings. "Would you rather hide and rely on Kalil to use common sense or compassion?"

"Bartholomew, you take me to the dining hall to get the guns and then show me how to get to the tower."

"On it, man." Bartholomew sprinted down the hallway.

"Here." Larson peeled off his brown leather bomber jacket and handed it to Jim. He pulled his Safari Adventure Company baseball cap off and plopped it down on Jim's head. "Wear these." He handed Jim his sunglasses. "It's a good thing you are so tall We are about the same size. Bartholomew will bring the others down when I am in place.

He handed Jim the radio. "If he gets impatient, you get on this radio and pretend you are me. Stall him. When the others arrive, you will know I am ready. You walk out slowly and take your time. Once he sees you, he will quit the countdown. When you hear the first shot fired, run like heck back to this monastery and don't stop until you get all the way inside to the church. Do you hear me?"

Jim and Sara nodded yes.

Larson turned to go, but Sara grabbed him and spun him around. She pulled his head toward her and kissed him solidly. Then she grabbed him by the shoulders and stood him up. "I love you, Larson," she said with her eyes misting up. "I have for a long time now. I couldn't tell you while I thought Kalil might kill my father. But, I want you to know that now."

"I love you, too, Sara," Larson said still shocked by the kiss-and-tell.

"Now get up in that tower and shoot this son of a bitch out of the sky!"

"Okay," Larson smiled blushing, his eyes darting at Jim.

"Hey, no kiss from me, but amen on the shooting part!" Said Jim smiling.

"This is going to be one incredible story, no matter how it turns out," Jim said to Sara as Larson raced down the hallway.

When it seemed that ten minutes was almost up, the voice called out from the helicopter again. Kalil barked over the speakers, "Larson, your time is up! Turn on the radio and tell me what is going on. Jim waited almost a minute, then he turned the radio on and used his roughest sounding Larson-voice. "They have located the others. Just hold your horses a minute and everyone will be here."

"I don't have to wait on you, Larson. I can just start shooting now. I will get what I want with or without you. I am only trying to be fair and let you walk out of here alive."

"We'll be out in just a minute. You are getting everything you want – give us just a minute." Jim flipped the radio off and shook his head.

Toussaint and Weinberg appeared just as Kalil began shouting into the microphone again. "Okay, we're coming out now," Jim faked his voice one more time into the microphone. Flipping off the switch, he turned to the others. "Is Larson all set then?"

"Yes," Toussaint said. "He was very happy to see such excellent rifle and ammunition for him to use. The gun he chose had a scope and what he called 'big fat armor-piercing' bullets. He sent Bartholomew back into the church, so everything is ready."

"Kalil is expecting us. Let's not keep him any longer." Jim started toward the entrance.

"Wait," Weinberg called out. He took Sara and Jim's hand, and they joined hands with Toussaint. "Dear God protect us. Thy will be done. Amen. Okay, I'm ready now. Let's go."

"That was short, Weinberg," Jim said as they walked out the door into the sunlight. "You sure didn't give God a lot of information on this thing."

Weinberg looked up at the sky as the three powerful helicopters spotted them and began moving closer. "He already knows, Jimmy. He already knows."

~~~

In the slender stone tower on the southern corner of the monastery wall, Larson kneeled at the arched window and looked out at the scene below. The rifle he held was okay but not what he'd have chosen for the job. Of course, the odds would be a lot better if he had been able to set the sight perfectly and actually practice with the weapon. But the situation was what it was. He had to now be incredibly perfect to pull it off.

The center helicopter descended lower than the others and prepared for a landing in the wide courtyard. The other two remained aloft and showed no intention of landing.

They must have taken off from somewhere in Turkey, he thought. Kalil had plenty of his buddies in that country. Enough, at least, to let three armed helicopters slip into a country patrolled by American, British, and French aircraft to secure the no-fly zone that was still in place to protect the other countries from Iraq's dangerous and aggressive dictator.

He slid his finger on the trigger ever so gently and waited for just the right moment. "If I shoot the helicopter that is landing first, the two above will see what is happening and attack. I will shoot each one of the two on top and hope it crashes into the lower one. If not, I will try to get it as fast as I can. At the very least, Sara and the boys should be able to get back inside before Kalil uses his machine guns. He may figure this out then and get me in this tower, but then he will be down to one helicopter – and that's better than three."

The four figures below moved cautiously into the opening. From this angle, Jim looked just like Larson. Everything was in place. Larson said a prayer, closed one eye and waited an extra moment for the helicopters to come just a bit closer. He drew a deep breath and held it to remain perfectly still when he fired.

~~~

Samangi had joined the Kurdish rebel militia opposing the vicious Iraqi government not long after the army had burned his village to the ground. Never again would he see the faces of the wife and children he hadn't even been given the privilege of burying. He had endured hardship, deprivation, and danger for over two years now. Still he fought on. What else was he to do?

Besides, the strategic raids they performed effectively in depleted the resources of the hated national army. He sometimes felt sorry for the men who had to die...but not too sorry. Perhaps some were even the ones who had killed his wife or two young daughters. Each time he destroyed their equipment, though, it gave him a sense of revenge and proper justice. He would fight on until death or victory came to Iraq.

But victory was a vague notion. With the odds so wildly in the favor of the well financed and trained government he didn't give much thought to an end to it all. Each day was a struggle to survive and to destroy. He embraced that with determination and ferocity.

It was exactly when their leader received word that three army attack helicopters had passed nearby from the North. They were already loading their weapons into the Land Rovers when they heard the first missile explosion over in the direction of the monastery. When they cleared the ridge and crawled to the edge he knew he would have an excellent shot. There the devils were, just hovering a few hundred meters away, facing the smoldering crater they'd just blown in the monastery.

Assembling the obsolete Soviet-made surface-to-air missile launcher with practiced care, he loaded the deadly missile into the back opening and snapped it into launch mode. Samangi took first aim at the helicopters. He'd never seen these models before. No doubt the dictator had invested millions of petro-dollars into the purchase of these sleek new machines. This would be better than most raids, the thought. The army usually avoided religious targets, and the monastery had been here for years. The monks inside had fed him and his companions many times. They were the ones who tended their wounds and, more than once, hid them from the army.

Now he had a chance to pay the monks back in a special way. Yes, this one would be satisfying indeed. The commander raised his hand. Samangi looked across the ridge at the five other men with S.A.M. launchers.

"You two shoot at the closest helicopter, you two shoot at the one on the outside and Samangi, you are the best shot, you kill the one in the middle," said the commander.

"On my signal, we fire," he shouted over the echo of the helicopter rotors. The Kurdish fighter cocked his head to one side and, based on his training, sighted the helicopter lowest to the ground.

The commander's voice rang out loud and clear, "THREE...TWO... "Wait - the marksman's eye flashed to movement at the side of the target, "what were those four people doing walking out in front of the monastery?" ...ONE...*FIRE!*"

~~~

Weinberg, Toussaint, Sara, and Jim walked four abreast toward the open area. Kalil's helicopter settled down slowly in front of them, ever closer. Now he could see Kalil's face in the passenger seat. He was gloating at his great fortune. How could these people be so stupid as to surrender to him? He would not let Sara get away this time. She would pay for the death of his bodyguard and the violation of his compound. Among the treasures he hoped to steal, she was one he would enjoy the most.

"Keep your eyes straight ahead," Sara cautioned. "Don't even think about turning around to look for Larson. If Kalil suspects that something is up, we are all dead where we stand."

Kalil looked closely at Jim, then leaned over to the pilot and said something. The back door of the helicopter slid open. Something was wrong.

The scene was just too unbelievable to take in. Jim turned his head to distract himself - braced for the unthinkable - determined to stand his ground until Larson fired the rifle. He scanned the sky and the hills in the distance. His eye caught the glint of metal on the mountain behind the helicopters and five puffs of smoke appeared in sequence. A sharp report rang out from the same spot a second later.

As if on cue, a gunshot popped from the monastery behind them. The higher helicopter on the right shuddered and wobbled, then began to shake violently. The second shot rang out just a fraction of a second later.

"Run!" shouted Weinberg to the frozen group. But before they could move, five vapor trails looped across the space between the mountain behind them and the helicopters. The first missile hit the chopper on the left, exploding it in a rainbow of sparks and flames. It sank to the ground like an anchor. The second missile sizzled past them and exploded farther down the mountainside.

The pilot had no time to report in on the radio before being obliterated, so Kalil was unaware of the destruction of the first helicopter. He was focused on the realization that Jim was not Larson. Sensing a trick, he commanded the pilot to fire the heavy machine guns directly into the four people on the ground. Just as the guns began to erupt, Weinberg, Sara, Toussaint, and Jim threw themselves to the ground. The gunfire would not last long. Jim looked up from the dirt just in time to see one of the three remaining hand-launched surface-to-air missiles slam into the tail of Kalil's helicopter, spinning it around so the guns fired away from the team. It crashed hard to the ground but was so close to the earth that it landed practically intact.

The fourth missile sailed past the targets. The fifth hit the remaining helicopter as it shuddered and swayed, its pilot already slumped over the controls with a bullet in his brain. Flashing into a brilliant orb of flame, the dead bird careened down on its side and headed directly for Kalil's helicopter below.

The soldiers inside the downed chopper leaped out of the machine and began to run before the ruptured fuel tanks could explode. Gunshots cracked out from the tower above in rapid succession, taking down the first two men who jumped out.

Kalil sprang to the ground and fired his automatic weapon into the tower in the direction of the gunfire. Kalil never had time to blink as eight tons of burning metal collapsed directly on top of him and exploded in a wild and thunderous maelstrom.

Jim covered his head and hunched his shoulders into the ground. He felt searing heat blast across his back. The smoldering burnt smell of his own hair as it singed off his arms and head reached his nose. When the fury subsided, the four members of the Safari Adventure Company helped each other to their feet and dusted themselves off. Speechless, they surveyed the three burning helicopters in front of them. No survivors, no more enemy. It was a miracle.

On the ridge in the distance, the Kurdish militia shouted, pumped their fists in the air, and hugged each other in victory. This was a six-million-dollar day!

Over the noise of the ripping flames came a highly excited voice from the tower. Larson was shouting "Hey! Hey! Hey! *DID YOU SEE THAT?*"

The Ancient Library

Moving the stones that Sylvus and his companions had placed at the entrance to the chamber was a lot more work than he thought it would be. Larson had declined the assistance of the monks that Brother Omar had offered. They had their hands full repairing the monastery, tending a wounded one, and preparing for a funeral. The Kurdish militia had offered their assistance in rebuilding the damaged wall, and would clear and bury the twisted wreckage in the courtyard when it cooled down enough to touch.

So after a night's rest, down into the cave they went, the five of them plus Bartholomew. Each had experienced the exhilarating feeling of gazing into the chamber through the missing stone. Now they were hard at work removing the wall in eager anticipation of what they would find inside. Although the work was hard, the mood was light and fun.

"Well, as the monkey said when he caught his tail in the lawnmower..." Toussaint kidded, "it won't be long now!"

Everyone chuckled at the bad joke. "That did not deserve such a gracious laugh, but today it gets one. Thank you," said Toussaint.

"Timing is everything, Weinberg," said Sara as she tossed another stone on the growing pile behind them. "This is a very good day indeed."

"Are you ready for this, Jim?" Weinberg asked privately when they sat down to take a drink of water and a short rest away from the others.

"Of course, I am ready. Aren't you?"

"Well, to be sure I am excited. And I guess, yes, since you've asked, I've prepared myself for whatever we find inside this chamber.

But have you considered what the implications of our discovery are in your personal life?"

"In what way?"

"You told me you came on this journey, refusing to go back to America when the bomb in Egypt should have sent you packing so you could get a shot at touching the archaeological proof of the faith I've been sharing with you since we met in Africa."

"Yes, that is why I started down this road," said Jim. "Now, after everything I've learned from you, Larson, Sol in Jerusalem, and here, I guess I've been pulled along by the momentum of what you believe."

"So where are you now?" Weinberg asked. "Is this an exercise in faith or a test of it?"

"You know, that is a good question, Weinberg."

"Here's what I am asking you to consider before you enter this chamber and before we open a single container. If we find authentic, verifiable proof of Jesus who you know very well existed, by some evidence in this chamber...I mean, if you get to see what no believer has ever seen, will you believe and become a Christian too?

"The second thing you need to consider is, what if we find nothing inside? What if this is like Sylvus's house on Akatori? What if the Library was moved or was never here, and you go the rest of your life without this proof? What will you do then?"

Jim sat and thought about these questions for a moment. "Weinberg, you are so great at putting things like this in perspective. Whatever happens, I hope you won't give up on me, and that we can be friends for a long time."

"I like you, Jimmy boy," said Weinberg laughing. "Yes, we will be friends for as long as you will have me." They shook hands.

"Then I guess the answer I have to give you right now is that I don't know what I am going to do. Honestly, either way I am going to have to trust my feelings and what I see. So if you have to have it on paper, this is a test of faith."

Jim stood to go back to work on the wall. "I will tell you, though, I really do *want* to believe with all my heart. The restlessness I have been experiencing since we left Africa is a burden I want to be relieved of. Hearing Sara read the manuscript up in the monk's library was an incredibly exciting experience. If I can find a scrap of faith in that chamber, then I am going to do everything within my power to believe."

"Hey you two! Get over here! I think we've got our way in!" Larson shouted. By the time they returned to the wall, Jim just caught sight of Sara crawling over a small pile of the stones that had fallen, following Larson and Toussaint into the chamber. Bartholomew helped the two men into the opening and followed them in himself.

"I brought the other battery-powered light," said Toussaint, setting up the lightweight aluminum tripod and flipping on the switch. The room glowed to life with the piercing blue-white light from the halogen bulb. There along the wall were lined up multiple clay jars each sealed neatly and, other than a fine layer of dust, in exactly the perfect condition they had been left in.

The team went right to work. Out came the collection instruments, flashes from the digital still camera from Sara, and footage from the video by Toussaint as the scientists went to work. When they were convinced they had mapped out the whole location, they were ready to open the jars. Sara admired the style of the jars, verifying the age and authenticity of them relative to what should be expected from the First Century Roman origins they promised to be.

Choosing the one closest to the door, Larson held the sides while Weinberg and Toussaint pried open the seal and lifted the top off, ever so carefully. When they all tried to look inside at once, they bumped heads, knocking Toussaint's helmet light off. "Here, get me some more light and let's take it easy, okay?" he smiled.

Toussaint peered into the jar and a wide smile moved across his face. "Ahh, will you look at this? Perfectly preserved!" He placed his rubber-gloved hand inside the jar and lifted out a scroll still neatly bound by a piece of linen cloth.

"What is it? What is it?" Jim asked.

"Sara, could you look at this?" Toussaint handed it to her. She was also wearing rubber gloves and placed the scroll gently into a collection tray. Shining her helmet light into the tray, she examined the piece carefully and said. "It appears to have the mark of the trading company owned by Sylvus that we've seen on some of the other documents and in his house in Greece!"

"Oh wow!" said Jim.

Bartholomew clapped his hands together and laughed. "Far, far, far out, sports fans!"

"YES!" Larson pulled a clenched fist into his chest.

Toussaint pulled seventeen more scrolls out of the jar, then declared it empty. He handed them to Sara who photographed them and placed them in different containers to be examined later.

"Well, what do they say?" Jim asked.

"It's not like that Jim. We don't pull them out and read them like a message in a bottle. These are very delicate, ancient, and fragile. I've seen documents like this, looking perfectly intact, vaporize into dust on contact. We will take them up to the monastery where the rest of the equipment is set up and analyze them there if they can be opened without special equipment."

"Okay, I see. I guess I've waited long enough, just knowing they are here is a fantastic discovery, isn't it?"

"Yes, this is truly amazing," Sara agreed, smiling first at Jim, then at Larson.

The men moved on to the second jar and repeated the opening. Lifting the lid and shining his light inside of it, Toussaint's mouth turned down at the corners. "This is strange," he said.

"What do you see?" Weinberg asked.

"Ashes."

"What?"

"Ashes, burnt carbonized ash. Nothing more. Here, Sara hand me that collection cup." He lowered the plastic ladle into the jar and pulled up a full scoop of black soot ash. "That is all there is in this one. Let's look at the next one."

For the next two hours, one by one each jar was opened to reveal the same small pile of ashes in the bottom. "Twenty-seven jars of ashes," Toussaint said. The tiredness in his voice revealed the disappointment they all felt. As the jars were being opened, Jim and Bartholomew had scouted the rest of the chamber for another passage or other containers. They had even gone back into the caves and searched around for more chambers.

Feeling empty-handed, tired, and disappointed, they gathered up the airtight plastic containers with the eighteen scrolls from the first jar and a marked sample of the ash from the second one, then made their way back to the monastery above.

Later that night, Brother Omar assembled the monks in the dining hall. The word had spread rapidly that the hoped-for relics of the Ancient Library were not found. Jim looked around at the peaceful faces of the brotherhood and thought how differently they behaved. How many of the people he knew would have endured the attack, the inconvenience, the destruction, and desecration of their home only to find that the reason some stranger asked them to sacrifice turned out to be not true? There would be a riot, and probably a lawsuit! Yet these monks chatted easily among themselves and continued to greet and treat the Safari Adventure Company members as honored guests. A few of the Kurd militia joined them and were treated with the same respect. The brave fighters rarely got much credit for their efforts. Tonight, they felt a soldier's pride. They were heroes here at the monastery.

Larson entered the room with Sara and Toussaint. Weinberg came over and sat next to Jim, patting him on the leg as if to console his disappointment, but smiling all the while. In many ways, in many good ways, he thought, the kind Englishman was just like these monks.

"Brothers and good friends from the Safari Adventure Company," Brother Omar stood before the group at the lectern in the main dining hall. The place was no worse for the trouble that had happened in the last two days. Order had been restored and business continued as usual. "We are now to be addressed by the chief translator of the archaeological team. Dr. Sara Einstein will share with us this evening what she has discovered relative to the four scrolls found in the chamber below the altar. Brother Bartholomew, our own chief translator, will change her English into our tongue for the many of us who do not speak her language. Dr. Einstein, please?"

Sara made her way up to the platform and opened her notes. She made some introductory remarks, mostly about the scientific nature of what she'd found, and what she'd done to maintain the documents. Most of the information was of little interest to the monks, but they sat politely and listened. It was not every day they had a woman speaker!

"The explanation of the ashes in the jars and the disappearance of the items we saw in the inventory that were part of the original collection is pretty clear. What I have here is my translation of the first scroll in the jar that was not burned." Everyone perked up to listen closer. Jim watched as she pulled a new page of notes and looked at them for a moment.

Sara cleared her throat and looked at the people looking back at her in anticipation. Her eyes drifted across the thousand-year-old monastery. It seemed to Jim as if she were spellbound by the moment.

"I…I guess I was thinking of all the people who had eaten here in this wonderful place throughout the centuries. What I have to share with you is a letter, never before seen by the world, from a man who sat at the feet of the Apostles and heard them teach firsthand the beautiful words of Jesus himself. He invested the rest of his life serving that ministry. And when the last of the Apostles was gone, he spent his entire fortune collecting their writings and preserving them. He alone was the caretaker to these treasures.

Sylvus of Akatori did indeed possess some of the writings of Jesus, a thing the world has never seen. He also had some of the Lord's final possessions including a walking stick and a bracelet Jesus wore. Most amazing of all, he had in his possession a painting of the Savior made during his ministry here on earth. He risked his life to gather these things, rescue them from certain destruction and bring them all the way here, then secure them in the cave below us, right here at your monastery.

"My words are secondary, however, to the letter he has written to us, to you, and in fact to the world. From this point on, I will read it word for word. You will understand the importance of this in just a few moments.

"'To the followers of Christ, here and abroad, and the brothers of the church of the monastery here in Assyria. I, Sylvus, write this letter to you as a final note before I return to the seaport and set sail for my home land.'"

Jim closed his eyes and concentrated on her voice. In his mind, he pictured Sylvus standing at the back rail of a ship sailing West back across the blue Mediterranean. He saw him with long white hair and beard, the sea wind blowing across his face and the setting sun in front of him. A wise man who had seen the apostles of Jesus first hand, and lived in the time of the people who had turned the world upside down.

"'By now you will have no doubt opened the jars of the collection I have brought here and found that they are empty save for the ashes in the bottom. As the caretaker of the sacred possessions of Jesus and the apostles, I am compelled of God to give you all an accounting of their fate. The scrolls and possessions I have spent my life and fortune, not one moment or penny which I regret, attracted an unforeseen problem as I moved them here. While I used to bring them to our secret worship services for the encouragement of the saints, the people who sought them grew more and more superstitious about their powers.

"'Stories were told of the healing power of a scrap of garment of an apostle. People claimed superstitious miracles were transferred from these possessions. The wildest tales were being told. People began to come to me, willing to pay money to touch or even glimpse the possessions. I will tell you now; it is a true statement, none of these items, even the bracelet of Jesus himself, had any supernatural power at all.

"'Though I pleaded this with the pilgrims who sought them, some traveling great distances, they fervently sought access with stories that were sometimes strange, and sometimes so sad they drove me to tears. It is a terrible thing to turn away a wife who believes you hold the cure for a disease that is killing her husband.

"'As I secured the collection and made my way secretly across the land, I continued to hear tales of unscrupulous men who had in their possession a lock of hair, a tooth, or bone, they claimed to be of an apostle. These men were boasting miraculous powers for their unhealthy possessions and, worse yet, charging money, often from the poorest people for the privilege of viewing or touching them. There were so many people claiming to be carrying a piece of wood from the cross of Christ that for them all to be true, the cross would have had to have been the size of Noah's ark! Still I guarded these sacred and true relics, as I felt led by God.

"'When I arrived here and met the brothers who were beginning the monastery, I inquired of their wisdom and prayed fervently for nearly a month as to the course I should take. The Lord revealed to me that if the existence of these beautiful and sacred things should be known, an uproar would be caused, greater lies would be told, and wars may even be fought for their control.

"'I feared as the scribes diligently copied the scriptures of the Apostles, that the originals I held so dear would become objects to be worshipped, instead of learning the meaning and the power of the words themselves, apart from the ink and material they lie on. Sadly, the destruction of these relics seemed the best course of action. In this jar, I have placed a list of the entire inventory and a precise copy of the book of Mark, which was told to him by the Apostle Peter. There are other items I have copied and recorded along with this. If the discovery of these things is delayed, I pray that they be used for the encouragement of the saints at that time, and for the glory of God.

"'By my own had did I, in tears and great sadness, set fire to the things that would burn. I gave the objects to common folks, and the bracelet of Jesus to a beggar who came near the cave last night. If I have learned anything in my journey to follow Christ in these difficult times, it is that faith is beyond that which we can touch and feel. And love is the earthly habit Jesus wanted most to teach. Love and faith begin with God, flowing through us if we are willing to accept them and then, and only then, can words become real things, in the actions of the people who love Him not for what he can do for them now, but what he's already done for them for eternity.

"'Finally, I must confess, that despite my strongest desire to avoid leading others astray to superstitiously worship powerless relics, I could not destroy the final item. For days I sat and gazed at the painting of Jesus. I prayed and fasted and sought to both comprehend, and separate the will of the Father from my own passion for the compelling image.

"'I knew that copies of the manuscripts were already abundant. There were already men and women of faith who had taken it upon themselves to memorize entire letters of the scriptures in perfection. I knew the Word would be sustained. The stick and the bracelet and other objects were simply that, objects. But the painting was haunting, piercing, and compelling. I saw Jesus only once. I will admit to my eternal shame that I listened to him for a while, scoffed, and returned to work.

"'Many had come preaching falsely in His name in my time. I was not seeking such a one in this simple teacher. When I look at this painting, the image seems to come to life. For you see, the artist, whom I do not know, captured as best one can, the indescribable nature of His eyes. Kind, loving, compassionate, wise, and pure, they reach out of the painting and move me. I will not take this painting back to Greece or Rome. I am not strong enough to either keep it secret or to keep it safe.

"'So I have chosen instead to give it to the monks who are building a monastery here. I have told them that the man in the painting was known simply as The Teacher in my land. They don't have much in the way of possessions or vestment for their ambitious little church here. They thanked me for this gift and promised to keep it as a reminder to always teach others.

"'This I do in full conscience of my commitment to God and to the Lord Jesus Christ. Grace and peace be unto you. Until the Lord returns.'"

Sara looked up from her notes. Her eyes were wet with tears. The room sat in absolute, transcendent silence. Jim opened his eyes and saw that many of the monks were weeping and praying. Then as if on cue, they began to look at each other, connecting with an unspoken realization that moved them to certain action. The chief Priest, Brother Omar, stood, bowed his head, and moved toward the sanctuary deep inside the mountain. One by one, each monk rose and followed him without a word. The members of the Safari Adventure Company watched them go, uncertain about what strange ritual might be occurring.

Bartholomew lingered at the door, turned, and motioned for Jim to follow. Jim got up and joined him and the others. Weinberg, Larson and Sara, and Toussaint entered the high-roofed church right behind Jim. The room had been reassembled, barely showing the effects of the missile blast that had knocked many of the paintings and decorations to the ground. But the priests were not paying any attention to the grandest of art works. They were standing reverently and staring at the smaller obscure painting called The Teacher.

The frame had been cracked where it had fallen to the floor when the explosion had hit. One of the many small fires that started had scorched the edge and a water stain had left shadow over the upper right hand corner. But there in all its simplicity and glory was the face of the only Son of God – much more than the greatest teacher who ever lived, but the living Word of Truth gently teaching those who took the time to listen.

Barely a word was spoken in the stone mountain sanctuary that night. Some knelt and prayed alone and in groups. Fresh candles were brought in to replace the ones that burned away in a vigil of illumination. As the hours passed, one by one, each left the sanctuary, returning to their small rooms to be alone with thoughts of the incredible day.

Only three remained, Weinberg, Bartholomew, and Jim. Jim asked them a thousand questions; they answered what they could.

He wept.

He prayed.

And some time as the night turned to dawn, not because of a painting or a scrap of tattered scroll, but through the power of the Holy Spirit, he asked Jesus to come into his heart and save his soul.

After the Crucifixion

But Thomas, one of the twelve called Didymous, was not with them when Jesus came.

The other disciples therefore were saying to him, "We have seen the Lord!" But he said to them, "Unless I shall see in His hands the imprint of the nails, and put my finger into the place of the nails, and put my hand into His side, I will not believe."

And after eight days again, His disciples were inside, and Thomas with them. Jesus came, the doors having been shut, and stood in their midst, and said, "Pease be with you."

Then He said to Thomas. "Reach your finger, and see my hands; and reach here your hand and put it into my side; and be not unbelieving, but believing."

Thomas answered and said to Him, "My Lord and my God!"

Jesus said to him, "Because you have seen Me, have you believed? Blessed are they who did not see, and yet believed."

Many other signs therefore Jesus also performed in the presence of the disciples, which are not written in this book; but these have been written that you may believe that Jesus is the Christ, the Son of God; and that believing you may have life in His name.

John 20: 24-31

Miracles

A song Barry Ochsner

I wish I could have been there,
I wish I could have seen,
All the people gathered 'round when they heard the
woman scream.
"I have touched His robe and I have seen his face!
Now I am a child of God,
My sin has been erased."

Try to imagine the excitement in the air,
When they went to the tomb and they found that He's
not there.
"Jesus is risen, God's plan is made complete.
And because of the victory on the cross, I will never
know defeat.

He performs miracles, I know without a doubt.
He awoke Lazarus, and he heard Peter shout.
And I didn't know the blind man, or watch Moses part
the sea,
But I am a first-hand witness to the miracles He's
performed in me.

To hear this entire song go to
http://www.SafariChronicles.com

ABOUT THE AUTHOR

Rick Butts is an author, professional speaker and entrepreneurial founder of businesses in electronics, manufacturing, financial services, and entertainment.

Growing up on a pig farm in rural Illinois, he moved to the Lake of the Ozarks, Missouri to attend high school. With his brother Randy he formed a rock and roll band playing bass guitar and vocals. Rick continued to play music professionally in touring bands, and in Las Vegas shows, for ten more years.

Rick ran a wooden-pallet manufacturing operation in St. Joseph, Mo. with his father, Ron Butts, who taught him much of his business sense - though it often wasn't easy to learn it from his dad!

When his daughter, Rachael, was born, Rick traded his guitar in for a suit and tie and a career in sales. Soon he opened a retail electronics business in Houston, Texas - the very first company to do mobile installations of automobile alarms - soon branching into cellular, audio and more.

While in the insurance and financial services field, Rick made a life changing decision to follow his passion to write and speak. He developed several training seminars on sales, leadership, and personal development. During this time he wrote the original Safari Chronicles: Volume 1which has sold more than 15,000 copies.

During this time, Rick attended Southwestern Baptist Theological Seminary and was the pastor of a non-denominational church near Houston.

Rick is a much sought after motivational speaker and marketing consultant. Living in Colorado and Arizona, he operates more than 20 Internet based businesses and appears internationally at conferences all over the world. For more information about having Rick speak at your meeting go to http://www.RickButts.com or call 800-442-6214.

NOTES

You can use this book as a study guide for your discussion group. This is best done by observing the main character Jim and his response to the people he meets and the things he sees.

What are they trying to teach him?

What can you learn from them for your own life?

NOTES

NOTES

To order additional copies of this book,

Call 800-442-6214 or http://www.RickButts.com

(We offer special volume pricing for study groups or gifts!)

ATTN: Speakers, Authors, Writers, and Entrepreneurs

Rick works with selected individuals who wish to increase their profitability through consulting, especially in the areas of developing creative and unique marketing strategies, and leveraging information products into multiple streams of income.

Referred to by his clients as "The Oracle" because he uses no forms, or specific systems, Rick brings a blank sheet of paper to every project and delivers breakthrough ideas that stand out and get results.

If you are interested, go to

http://www.RickButts.com/oracle

or email
rick@RickButts.com